My Opinion

My Opinion

Mac Mall

© 2015 Mac Mall
All rights reserved.

ISBN: 0692456570
ISBN 13: 9780692456576

*This book is dedicated to
Big Mama and Big Daddy*

FORWARD BY MAC MALL

I WROTE THIS BOOK after my accident. As I recuperated and pondered my existence. I'm sure if it wasn't written I would surely dead or in a psychiatric institution.

Being able to step back examine my life allowed me to exercise demons that haunted my soul for as long as I could remember. It's a blessing that I'm here to tell the tale of this wild journey called my life. I would like to thank all those who accompanied me along the way family, friends, lovers, and haters all of you played a key part in my life and in this story.

To the person who reads this book, first I thank you for taking time out of your life read my story. I pray that you learn from my all my up and downs and take head to my many mistakes. They say a wise man doesn't learn from his mistake he learns from the mistakes of others. So read this book, learn from this book, and don't make the same mistakes as I did. Thank you

My birth certificate was forged, my name was misspelled and I always hated Mondays.

CHAPTER 1

This certifies that Jamal Diallo Rocker was born to Shirley Marie Davis in this hospital at 2:08 a.m. on Monday, June 14, 1976.

I always tripped on this, because the good people at the hospital misspelled my name—plus, I always hated Mondays. As you can see, this certificate has been altered right here where my last name is. You see, my real last name is Esters, due to the fact that my biological father's last name was Esters. Well, I shouldn't say my "father," because he never raised me. Shortly after I was born, he left Vallejo for good, abandoning my mother and me because my mother wouldn't pack up and move to Chicago.

You see, the man who fertilized the seed that would later become me was what some call a ladies' man or what others call a player. But in my opinion, he was just plain loose. Besides my mother, he was involved with about two or three other women in Vallejo and had a couple of kids out of state. My mother knew that if he got around like this in Cali, it could only get worse if we got on his home turf, so she didn't go. Later in life, she would tell me that when I was born, she realized that she didn't live for herself anymore, and her first responsibility was to me, so she wasn't about to gamble our lives on a relationship that was best described as shaky.

Shirley was from the small town of Vallejo, but she was by no means naïve. She was the seventh of thirteen children and raised with a strong sense of family values that she got from her parents, Catez and Ida Davis, both of whom were hardworking natives of Louisiana.

My grandmother, Big Momma, loves to talk about how she used to work from sundown to sundown when she was young—you know, in the field, picking cotton. Sometimes she picked a couple of hundred pounds a day for pennies. One of the reasons she was interested in my grandfather, Big Daddy, was that he didn't pick cotton; he cut puck-wood trees.

See, Big Daddy was a man's man. We didn't call him Big Daddy just because he was my mother's father; we called him that because of his stature. He stood about six four and was a solid three hundred pounds. You could tell just by looking at him that his African blood wasn't diluted by the slave masters who raped our ancestors back in the bad ol' days. His skin was black like the coal that diamonds come from and shiny like patent leather. He was a simple, honest man who believed that a man's worth lies in how hard he works. So he did just that to provide for his eleven girls, two boys, and beautiful wife. His deep, intense eyes told the story of pain and injustice that only a black man raised in the hate-filled South can tell. He had the hands of a person who had been doing manual labor since he could walk. I always thought that Big Daddy had some type of regalness about him like a Watusi king.

Man, they don't make 'em like that anymore! He left Louisiana to escape the racist South and to improve life for him and his family. He heard that there were a lot of well-paying jobs in California and felt that there was no way that he and his family would encounter the same hate in California that they endured in the South. So they moved to Vallejo, a city in the North San Francisco Bay Area. First they lived in Chabot and then in Floyd Terrace before settling in the Country Club Crest, an all-black middle class community that many people from Louisiana had migrated to.

The theory behind the Country Club Crest was positive: affordable homes, nice schools, and a quiet all-black community. That was the idea, but it quickly evolved into the hub for blacks all over Vallejo and became a place where one could sign up for the Panthers or even score some heroin. Back in the day, the turf had one way in and one way out. If you didn't know anybody and weren't buying dope, for sure it was a dangerous place to be. And if you were foolish to funk with a male or female from the Crestside (as it later came to be known), you had big problems. See, you fight one, you fight 'em all. Yeah, they were few, but they were crazy. When my mother got out of the hospital, this is where I was brought.

We lived at Big Momma and Big Daddy's house. My birth was a big deal, because they thought I was gonna be the last boy born into my family. All I really remember about those days is the love that I felt from my family. Now, I never really felt the loss of my biological father, because Big Daddy, the other men in my family, the women, my aunts, and my cousins damn near spoiled me. Once my mother got on her feet, we moved to Capitol Street in Vallejo. That's just about the time she met my real father, Eric David Rocker, a man from the East Coast who was in the navy and stationed in San Francisco. He met my mother at a club in Oakland on the dance floor doing "the worm." He says that once he saw her and talked to her, he knew that she was "the one." Damn, that must have been one hell of a dance!

Eric married my mother and raised me as his own son. As a matter of fact, years later when my little brother was born, some wanted him to name him Eric Jr., but since he felt that I was his first son, he didn't do it; he named him Immanuel. I always loved and respected him for that. Since my pop was in the navy, we did a whole lot of traveling. I once lived in Alaska for two years; it was crazy.

When he got out of the navy, we came back to the Crest at Big Momma's house to settle into civilian life. In the first couple of years, things were really cool. My parents both got jobs, my pops at Chrysler and my mom at a convalescent home. Big Momma's was getting kind of crowded, you know, with fifty-two grandkids and twenty-two great-grandkids, you always knew somebody was gonna be on the couches or in one of her six rooms. You see my folks, the Davises, belonged to one of the biggest families in the 'hood. I had relative on almost every single street. While my mom and pops were getting things together, we lived on Mark Street with my Aunt Ruby and my cousin Yvonne. It got kinda hectic around this time, because my pops lost his job and my mom almost got killed in a car wreck. Then she tore her back up when a gurney broke while she was saving an old man at her job, so she wasn't working. When shit got bad, it really got bad!

People handle stress differently. My mom had the family to have her back, my pops chose alcohol, and I just drowned myself in music. My little brother was little, but I'm sure at that time, he had a lot on his mind. Music always played a big part in my life, whether it was the spirituals Big Momma sang in the kitchen, the down-home blues my Auntie Ruby played when the Hennessy started flowing, or the R&B and funk my mother played when she was cleaning up the house.

Music ran through my veins like blood—real talk. If music ran through my veins like blood, then hip-hop was my heart, and the classic record "The Message" by Grand Master Flash and the Furious Five was the song that made it beat. But don't get it twisted—I thought "Rappers Delight" by The Sugar Hill Gang was dope, but it was kind of pop, you know. Now, "The Message" was real; it was what I saw every day in the turf. If journalists had the label "gangta rap" back then, "The Message" would have been the first gangsta rap.

Whenever I heard it, I would get a warm feeling in my chest that would get hotter and hotter until I couldn't help but rap the verses word for word. Some people say they feel this way when they fall in love for the first time. Well, I believe them, 'cause when I was introduced to hip-hop and rap, I knew that it would be my first and only true love. I used to break-dance, pop lock, write graffiti, and all that. The first tapes that I ever got were a gift from my grandmother on my father's side, Juanita Rocker. They were Whodini, Fugitive, and Run DMC's Rock Box. I guess that was the beginning of the end of any dream my parents had of me being a doctor or a lawyer, 'cause I was gonna be an MC—that's right, a rapper. Microphone in my hand, beats slammin', and crowd under my control, doing whatever I wanted them to do. The only problem with that was that was at the time, I was super shy and stuttered every time I tried to talk. I still wrote raps, though, waiting for the day when I would get my chance to shine.

On the home front, things weren't goin' smoothly. I spent most of my time at my Auntie Mary Jean's house, kickin' it with my cousins Pug and Shanda. Auntie Mary Jean treated me like a son, and Shanda and Pug treated me like a brother.

Since my mom and pops were still trying to get on their feet, I moved to Mary Jean's house. That house was dope; I had my own bed with Donkey Kong sheets, and she always had four or five boxes of the best cereal for breakfast and plenty of good food to eat every night. Mary Jean lived on Gateway, one of the hottest streets in the Crest. I watched cats who would later become turf legends out there getting their money. I actually saw the game go from weed and hop to the almighty crack cocaine. Gateway in '85 was like the California gold rush, and crack was gold. Many cats made big names for themselves, but many died nameless.

Around that time, I heard Too Short for the first time. One of my cousins had played me a custom-made tape that Too Short had made for one of his baller patnas in Oakland.

When he came out with "Don't Stop Rappin'" on the 75 Girls label, it was a wrap. Bye-bye, Run DMC, hello, Playboy Too. Short Dogg was the godfather of this Bay Area rap thing and one of the pioneers of West Coast hip-hop in general. Where would life be if there was no Too Short, and there was nothing but rappers from the old New York? I would be trippin' if I didn't mention the two Bay Area cats Magic Mike and Calvin T. from up out of Richmond, California. If it wasn't for them, there surely wouldn't be Mac Mall. Snoop and Big Bill was the first ones to ever let me hear their songs, and I was turned out. These cats was the first pimps on wax. I'm talking about the genuine article.

Everybody in the Bay who rapped well borrowed from both these players, whether they know it or not. Between them—Too Short, Ice T, Big Daddy Kane, Kool G Rap, King Tee, and NWA—I knew I didn't just want to make words rhyme; I wanted to manipulate the English language in order to inform the masses of the cruelty of the inner city areas of America. Nah, for real, I wanted to "Spit Game!"

Life back then was fly. I mostly hung out with my patnas, Bird and Lonnie, and with my older cousin Pug's friends.

Thanks to Big Major, Dubee's daddy, I was able to play Pop Warner football and Little League baseball. Big Major hooked up me and a lot of other kids from the Crest whose parents weren't able to spend the money on sports. (That was real cool—thanks, Big Major!).

Besides being poor and on welfare (which you never really noticed, 'cause everybody else was too) and my pops drinking (which was getting worse), I had a lot of fun in school. Elementary went by quick, and I graduated Elsa Widenmann in the sixth grade. I started the seventh grade at Solano Junior High. Solano was wild. I finally got to go to school with Pug and the rest of my older cuddies, and the girls in junior high were way more fly than elementary. And when I found out I could cut class, it was too much for me to handle, so I flunked the seventh grade. I didn't really trip, 'cause two of the best things in my life that happened that year. First, the cuddies from the turf and I created the Ses Crew, a younger version of the Romper Room, who was making big noise in the 'hood back thing.

The second thing was that Mr. Michael Robinson (a.k.a. The Mac) came into my life. Straight up, The Mac was my hero.

Some fools thought Jordan was dope, but the only Mike I wanted to be like was The Mac. I remember The Mac from back in the day. He lived on Leonard Street. He was always into music, and I used to see him riding a moped with speakers on it. Plus, he was always rappin'. But back then when I was introduced to him, he had come all the way up.

He was the star rapper on one of the first independent record labels in the Bay, Strictly Business Records.

The label was owned by Renald Powers, Rick Nelson, and Khayree Shaheed. The Mac had the flow, Renald and Rick had the money and power and Khayree made the tracks. It was the perfect combination. They dropped The Mac's first album The Game *Is* Thick, and The Mac was at my junior high passing out posters. He had just started talking to one of my girl cousins, Larea, and when he saw me and her little sister, he asked us if we wanted a ride to the turf. We said yeah and hopped in his clean white Cadillac. This dude had so much beat in his trunk that when I sat in the backseat, I thought the speakers would crack my chest. He dropped us off, gave us one of his posters, and told me that when I had my raps together, I should come see him. When he told me that, I was on cloud nine with silver-dollar eyes. The Mac was the man, and he was one of the first people to give me encouragement with my rappin'.

I didn't really get much at home. I was livin' back with my mom on Mark Street. We were on welfare, and my pops was still hittin' the bottle, so I spent most of my time on the block with the Sesame Street. Back then, we were about twenty-four deep and lookin' for nothing but trouble. The Crest was on fire back then. You had us (the Sesame Street), the Grannys Boys, and the Crew Thang putting it down on Taper Street.

Also, the Romper Room was puttin' it down on Leonard Street and Sawyer.

It was on Sawyer Street that I saw Andre Hicks (a.k.a. Mac Dre) for the first time. He ran close with Ray and Ronnie Wags and my cousin Li'l Nate. Mac Dre would also be in front of Ray and Ronnie's grandfather's house on Leonard Street so Leonard Street stayed poppin'. Around this time, Mac Dre signed to Strictly Business Records and dropped the Bay Area classic, "Young Black Brotha." I was hella juiced, because now we had two rappers from my neighborhood. The Mac was political, and his raps came from the side of the OG baller—you know, like the connect. I guess some of that rubbed off on him from Rick and Renald, who both were giants in the game back then.

And Mac Dre was more street and grimy. He rapped from the side of the young black brothas out there grinding, riding Chevys, smoking weed, drinking Hennessy, and just trying to survive.

To me, both of them playas were all that and a crack sack. Even though there were a lot of crews in the Ses, we all moved as one. We didn't get along with anybody. If you weren't with us, you were against us. We didn't even get along with other fools from North Vallejo. We funked with the Hillside, South Vallejo, Millers Ville, downtown—whoever! Basically it was the Crest against the whole Vallejo. We didn't care, though. Matter of fact, we liked that shit. Suckas would say "fuck the Crest," but they couldn't fuck with the Crest.

In every ghetto, you've got at least one DJ. Ours was Cecil Allison (a.k.a. DJ Cee). Ceese, as we called him, was a Crestside OG. When anybody from Vallejo was having a party and wanted it to "jump," they got Ceese. He was cool as a fan and all about his music. He lived on Sawyer Street, and when I would walk from Big Momma's house, I used to see him in his room window on the turntables making a mix tape or just practicing. Ceese always threw dances at The Boys Club, which we called The Nenals, short for Continental Omega Boys Club. Anyway at this one dance I will never forget, the gym at The Boys Club was packed. The whole 'hood was there, plus some other turfs from North Vallejo, like Lofus and College Park.

Sometimes Ceese would let people grab the mic if he was feeling generous. On this particular night, a dude from College Park was rappin'. Now, at the time, my turf never tripped off College Park, because they were a small 'hood and really weren't a threat, but at junior high, my crew, the Sesame Street, chose them as enemies—probably because there was no one else to funk with. So this dude was rappin', givin' it up for the Park, when Freaky D, a cuddie from The Romper Room and Sawyer Street, grabbed me and asked me if I wanted to get on the mic. I said yeah, even though I was hella nervous. So Freaky D walked onstage and asked Ceese if I could get on the mic. I'll never forget it. He whispered in Ceese's ears, and Ceese looked at me for what it seems like an eternity. Then he waved me up on the stage. When my cuddies from my crew saw me onstage, they rushed the front of the stage. Other people paid attention mostly out of curiosity, I think. I mean, they knew me from runnin' with the Sesame Street, but that was it. So not many outside me crew and a few Crest OGs knew what to expect. On the real, this was gonna be the first time I actually ever touched a microphone in my life. Forget butterflies—I had bald eagles in my stomach.

But when homeboy finished his flow and Ceese put the microphone in my hands and all eyes were on me, I felt whole, complete. No shyness, no stuttering—it was natural. I mainly freestyled about the Crestside and the crew, and I mentioned a couple of D boys I knew but man, I was flying high. This was better than scoring a touchdown, better than making a three-point shot with no time left on the clock, straight up. I don't know if it was because my 'hood was in the building or if everyone was just surprised to see me rippin' it, but the crowd was hype. When I got off stage, folks were givin' me dap, and the cuddies from the crew were wildin' out, 'cause they knew that for the rest of the night, the girls were gonna be ridin' our dicks.

It was later that week that I got my name Mac Mall. In my 'hood, the name Mac carries a lot of weight. They don't just give you the name unless you're something special. See, you had Chris Macabee, a Crest OG, The Mac, Mac Dre, and Mac Lee, one of the dopest rappers in the 'hood and a member of the Crew Thang. And now, you had me, Mac Mall. I felt blessed.

The year I came back to repeat the seventh grade was a joke. I spent those days writing raps and being a bully with the Sesame Street. When the talent show came around that year, we decided to make our presence known, so Dubee, the whole crew, and I made Tshirts with "Sesame Street" on them and the words "College Park" crossed out. The day we went to school, we shocked it, but soon as we came through the doors, the principal rounded us up and suspended us for having gang colors on.

While we were on suspension, the crew and I went up to the school and beat down some of our rivals, and they expelled all of us except for Dubee, probably because of his father's influence. Since I was the youngest, I had to go to a continuation school called Best in West Vallejo, while the other cuddies got to go to Peoples, a continuation school in North Vallejo.

Before I started Best, I tried my hand at selling dope. I got some pretend crack from a friend of mine, risked my life, and sold it to a fein. I took the twenty dollars to one of my cuddies on Sawyer Street, and got "plugged" with a hundred-dollar sack. Honestly, I never liked selling "D." I mainly grinded for stuff I needed, like coats and shoes, 'cause like I said, my family was on welfare, but being a "D" boy wasn't for me.

MY OPINION

The Mac got killed in '91 in a case of mistaken identity. My cousin Larea, who was pregnant with Mac's son at the time, was in the car with him. The shooters told her to get out of the car, and then they shot Mike. It was a great loss. I cried like a newborn at his funeral. It hurts me even to this day. At that same funeral, Mac Dre's cousin, Carlos, had brought his patna from Santa Rosa, Ray Luv, to meet Mac Dre and Khayree. I didn't meet Ray then; I first heard him on a song that he and Mac Dre did. I finally met Ray when Kilo Kurt from the Romper Room Crew invited me to the studio where Mac Dre was recording his second record, What's Really Going On. I thought I was going up there to rap, but when I got there, Dre was finishing a song that he and Ray had did, so I was heated.

Kilo introduced me to Ray, and I gave him a kind of half-assed dap and kind of sat there and mugged him. He had on a red "9th and Link" hat, a red shirt, and a big-ass gold "R" ring on his finger. I'll be the first to admit that I was playa hating, but I thought that he was tryin' to take my spot, and I couldn't have that. Mac Dre was putting together Romp Records with Kilo Kurt. PSD, a rapper from the Crew Thang, was going to be their first artist, and I was going to be their second.

Kilo hooked up a session at Mac Dre's four-track studio after T Love and a couple of cats from my crew scraped together some paper and paid them so that I was overjuiced. I practiced my raps the whole night before the session; I even cut school that day. So when the time came, Mac Dre had played me some beats and was ready for me to record, but when I tried to rap, my mind went blank. I couldn't remember one line I ever wrote. I tell you that Dre and the rest of the cats at the studio talked bad to me—so bad that on the next day, I came to the studio and had my shit correct.

I made about six songs that day—cuts like "Versitile," "Pay This Pimp," and "Young in the Game." That was my first demo, and I was proud of it. The demo got around Vallejo, and my name was starting to ring. My crew was putting it down in the turf, so the rappin' was like icing on a cake. I thought I was on my way.

Well, that's what I get for thinking, 'cause soon after my demo dropped, Mac Dre, Kilo Kurt, and Jamal Diggs got set up by a rat and got sent to the feds for conspiracy to commit bank robbery. Just as I thought I was about to get on, it all got snatched away from me. I was through with money; I couldn't believe that it was real. The Mac was gone, and Dre was in the feds. It made me start to believe that rappin' wasn't for me. So I sold a little dope and hit a couple of licks to survive.

I still had dreams of rapping, but reality bites like a pit bull, so I hustled. It's funny how God works, 'cause I remember walking up Sawyer Street with Sleep Dank and talkin' about quittin' rappin' when DJ Ceese called me to his window and told me that Khayree wanted to hook up with me and my parents, because he wanted to sign me and start a label called Young Black Brotha Records.

Big Mama and Big Daddy in one of their first pics, I love and miss them.

Moms pregnant with me

MY OPINION

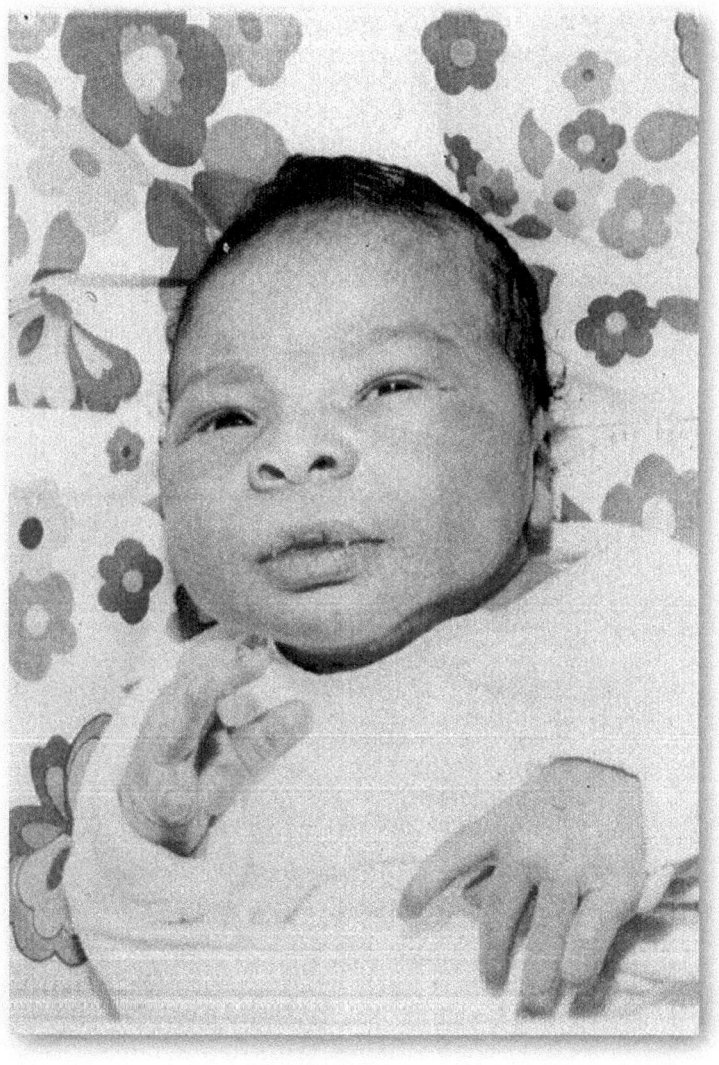

Baby Jamal

Michael Robinson "The Mac" the man that let me know all my dreams could come true.

MY OPINION

Andre Hicks "Mac Dre" the cuddie that helped
me make my dream come true.

MAC MALL

DJ Cee, if it wasn't for Ceese I wouldn't have been able to get my deal. He made it possible for my dream to come true.

CHAPTER 2

When Ceece told me Khayree wanted to holla at me about signing to a new label he was starting called Young Black Brotha Records, I had mixed emotions. On one hand, I was superjuiced, 'cause in my opinion, Khayree was and is a genius. His music is how the Crestside streets sound. I knew that if we hooked up, I would become a part of a legacy, but on the other hand, I was havin' a run of some real buzzard luck. It seemed like nothing was going my way. I would get close enough to touch my goal, and the rug would get snatched from under me. A part of me thought this time would be no different.

Khayree was like a myth to me then. I never saw him hangin' out; I just heard and felt the passion in his music. He definitely had his finger on the pulse of the Country Club and the whole Bay with the records he made for Strictly Business.

One of the things that eased my mind was Ceese telling me that it was real business. Ceese was family; my mother used to babysit him way back when. He was always straight up and honest, so to me, his word was his bond. I got Khayree's number from Ceese, went directly home, and called him. We talked two or three times, but they were only short conversations, because Khayree was as busy as a dope dealer on the first. Between his campaigning to free Mac Dre, who had been railroaded by the feds and Ray Luv, who was signed to Strictly Business and dropped the Bay Area classic "Get Ya Money On," Khayree didn't have much time to chat on the phone. He told me he would come to the Crest to chop it up with me face to face and would probably bring some tracks, so I had to be ready to spit.

When the day arrived, a few cuddies and I were posted up in front of my house on Mark Ave. Khayree pulled up in his dark-blue BMW. We knew it was him, 'cause not too many cars like that came through the turf. My crew knew Khayree was in the 'hood to talk business with me, so they left me there in front of my house. My first impression of Khayree was that he was taller than he looked on the record covers and TV, and he wasn't mean muggin'; he was actually smiling. So I put my best cold-as-the-North-Pole face on and gave him some dap, and then he ran down his plans on how he was creating YBB (Young Black Brotha) Records. He really didn't have to sell me on the idea, though, 'cause I was a jump, skip, and a hop from a cell block or a pine box, so I felt I had nothing to lose.

Khayree had heard me rap on the four-track demo tape Mac Dre had produced for me, but I guess he wanted to hear me flow live to find out if my skills were actual and factual. I think this is where the man upstairs who controls all game stepped in, 'cause the first piece of music he played for me was knockin', and I must say, the rap I spit felt tailor made for the beat. The track and rap ended up being the title track to what would become my debut record Illegal Business. After I spit a few raps to a couple different beats, I guess Khayree was convinced, so we agreed we would make Young Black Brotha Records a reality. The next step, though, would be a hard one. We would have to persuade my parents to let their fifteen-year-old son get involved with strangers in a business they knew little, if anything, about.

My relationship with my pops wasn't too cool at this time. We barely even spoke, so I felt he would be against it or wouldn't care. My mom was under a lot of stress 'cause of the funk between me and my pops, and all she heard about the music business were horror stories of people getting strung out on drugs or dying broke because the record company robbed them. Plus, with the way I was livin' at that time, she could have thought only the worst.

Ceece set up a meeting at my house with him, Khayree, my parents, and me to discuss my future in the record industry. You should have seen us: Ceece and Khayree were sitting on the couch looking like they just stepped out of a rap video, and my folks and I were on the other side of the couch looking like we just stepped out of a episode of "Good Times."

My parents asked the usual questions like how this would affect me in school, who would look out for me and make sure I wouldn't fall victim to drugs, and what was up with the contract (who got what, how much, and when). Since I was a minor, a parent would have to sign along with me. For that reason, I was worried; if my pops told my mom not to sign out of spite, maybe mom wouldn't sign just to keep things cool between them. If that went down, I was right back where I started: the bottom of the bottom.

After Khayree finished his presentation, Ceese assured my parents that he would look out for me as best as he could, acting as DJ/mentor. Like I said, Ceese was family. After Ceese and Khayree bounced, my parents let me know that they thought I shouldn't risk my future on a dream and that I should concentrate on school. Then they informed me that if I disobeyed them and chose a music career, I would be doing so alone and without their support.

When they told me that, it really fucked me up. I mean, this was one of the biggest decisions in my life, and not having them have my back felt like they disowned my anyway. My mind was made up—matter of fact, it was a no-brainer.

My mom and pops wanted me to focus on school, but Hogan High School, which I was attending then, was just the minor leagues of the Crest against the rest of Vallejo funk. There, I focused only on the fighting with the enemy and smoking weed with the cuddies, and getting a name for myself was more important than studying or homework. My parents didn't want me to risk my future on a dream, but my life was at risk every day I woke up and went outside. I felt the music industry couldn't be worse than growing up in the 'hood.

Pops had washed his hands of the situation, so I was able to convince my mother to sign the contract. I had to promise her that I would finish school and stay out of trouble. I gave her my word, we both signed, and it was official: Mac Mall was the first artist signed to YBB. Then, it was more of a concept than an actual company, because Strictly Business Records was still running at full speed.

Even though The Mac was "Crestin' in peace," and Mac Dre was in Lompoc Federal Correctional Institute, the cat Ray Luv was keepin' it movin'.

His single "Get Ya Money On" from the EP Who Can Be Trusted had the Bay on lock; I mean, Ray was doin' it live.

He recorded remixes for Janet Jackson and En Vogue. Dude had shows almost every day of the week—sometimes two a day.

At one of these double hitters, Khayree, who had wanted to get me familiar with the rap life, brought me along. The first was a lowrider car show at a Manteca water park, and the second show was at a club in Vallejo called Talk of the Town. The Low Rider show was crackin'; it was hella superbad hinas there! N2Deep was headlining, ridin' high on their single "Back 2 the Hotel," and Mike Lott, a cuddie from the turf, was their hype man.

When he saw me backstage, he passed me a blunt and made me feel right at home. Lott located Ray Luv in his dressin' room, where he was posted with DJ Cee and Ant Dog, his right-hand man. Ray was shinin'—I'm tellin' you, shinin' like brand-new rap money. He had a no fear, a smile from ear to ear, and the confidence of a bullfighter. Ray Luv was no doubt fittin' in nicely with his new swagger. We kicked it for a while, and when it was time for Ray to go onstage, he handed me a mic and asked me if I wanted to go onstage. Hell yeah, I wanted to go onstage! I must have grabbed the mic out his hand, and I ran out on the stage so fast that I beat him out there.

When Ceese dropped "Get Ya Money On," the crowd went nuts. Man, the girls were lovin' it. They didn't even know who I was, but since I was onstage with a mic in my hand and rollin' with Ray, I guess that was enough for them. I got the star treatment; girls were pullin' on my pant legs, screaming, waving, and winking. Yeah, this was for me; I knew this was what I was supposed to be doing.

After the show at the water park, Ray told me I did well and asked me if I wanted to do the other show at the Talk of the Town in Vallejo. I wanted to, but I knew my parents wouldn't be too fond of that idea. See, I was only fifteen and the Talk of the Town was a twenty-one-and-over club. I couldn't let that get in my way, though. I told my parents I was spending the night at my best friend, Bird's, house, went home, and got dressed while they were out shopping. Then I ran around the corner to Ceese's house and got a ride to the club. Now, the club wasn't anything new to me; the crew used to parking-lot pimp in the front while waiting for it to let out.

So, all the faces was the same; it just felt like they looked at me different. Cuddies was in there buying me drinks (don't forget, I was only fifteen years old!). Man, grown women were speaking to me. "Shit," I thought, "if this is what I have to look forward to, bring it on!"

This night was important also, because I met Miss Leila Steinburg. Leila stood out in the crowd, not only because of her color—a mix of Mexican, Turkish, Polish, and Jewish—but because she was like a busy bee all around the club, making sure everything and everybody was taking care of. Ceese had told me she was Ray's manager, so I watched her handle business the whole night.

After we performed, I knew this was when God stepped in again, because something just came over me. I walked up to Leila and said, "My name is Mac Mall. I'm Khayree's new artist, and you gonna be my manager." It was an awkward moment, 'cause she looked at me as if I were crazy, but she gave me her number anyway and told me to give her a call so that we could talk and see if we were even on the same page. I would later find out that she was a teacher, a wife, and a mother of three daughters in addition of being Tupac's manager before he got with Digital Underground. Well, if it was good enough for Tupac, it was good enough for me, so I wouldn't take no for an answer. Leila being my manager was meant to be. I guess it was her mothering side that I liked about her, since my mom wasn't involved in my career. Leila and Ray welcomed me with open arms.

Ray even said he would let me be in the video to "Get Ya Money On," so I was amped. Khayree took me to the spot in Frisco where they were filming. Rick and Renold from Strictly Business were there. Ray Luv and the Link Crew, Ant Dogg, and Young Grin were there, blazin' up blunts and drinkin' Hennesy. Leila was runnin' around like crazy, making sure everything was straight and the film crew was ready to go. Being able to see the process of making a video was cool, but I felt a funny vibe in the building. I kind of felt like Rick and Renald didn't want me to be there.

What I didn't know was that when Khayree decided to form YBB, Rick and Renold wouldn't be involved. I always assumed they would be a part of the company, but that wasn't how it was gonna be. It was like they were looking at the little nigga who was gonna be the death of

Strictly Business Records. When I got hip to the whole get down, I had conflicting feelings. My first feeling was that this was my chance: all the opportunities I thought I had were taken away from me, and I wasn't about to let this one get away. But my other feeling was that I didn't want to be the reason Strictly Business Records broke up. They'd been through enough with The Mac getting killed and then Mac Dre getting set up; the last thing they needed was the producer of the company running off with me and doing his own thing.

After the video, I let Khayree know how I felt, and he told me that the split was due to creative differences; he wanted to have a label where he called the shots musically, and business wise, you can't fault a man for wanting his own. So I was with him: "Man, let's get that paper!"

So Khayree started giving me tracks, and we began putting together what would become my first record, Illegal Business. Leila agreed to be my manager, and with Dre in the feds, Ray took on a big cuddie role, letting me come along with him and perform at clubs and concerts. I felt like things were starting to happen—until Ray Luv caught a bullshit case and had to go to San Quentin for a ninety-day op.

Leila spent a lot of time trying to make sure he didn't get washed in the legal system and catch some serious time. Khayree was still shooting me tracks for the records, and I was writing up a storm. In the Crestside, the streets were on fire; it was like cats stopped grinding and started robbing banks. Every neighborhood Dboy switched his pitch up and became a modern-day Jesse James. Cuddies were runnin' up in every bank and credit union around. Some licks were so sweet, cats hit the same spot twice. This was the time some key members of my crew went down, mostly for robbery charges.

At first, the turf took the fed as a joke, but soon nobody would be laughin'. The 'hood lost some real soldiers to the funk, which was getting deeper by the day. With all this shit jumpin' off around me, it definitely influenced my rhymes.

My family had decided to take a vacation to Detroit that summer to go see my grandmother, Juanita Rocker.

Juanita was a strong, strict, smart woman. She invested in real estate and owned property throughout Detroit. I spent a lot of summers in Motown helping repair houses and doing other business. I couldn't see it then, but now I appreciate the knowledge I received while I was out there.

But this summer in particular, I wasn't trying to go out there. I had some Khayree beats to write to, the cuddies from the Strictly Ses (which we changed our name to) and I were putting it down in the town. I was right there in the middle of it. I wasn't trying to miss any of the action. But after my mom made me go, the trip was actually cool. I got a chance to step back from my reality and put together some real raw material for my CD.

When I got back to the Crest, it was on. Khayree had the game plan made and was ready to execute. He decided we were gonna call the record Illegal Business, since that was one of the first and tightest songs we made. We were gonna do a savage record cover, where I would be lookin' like I was plotting a heist. When I heard that, I was with it, but the next thing he said threw me off. He told me he wanted to add another L to my name, 'cause he didn't think people would get Mall from Mal. At first I didn't want to do it, but trick it! I was getting in the game, so that's all that mattered.

When I started my sophomore year at Hogan High, I was hyphy—I mean, I was experiencing stuff no teenager or most adults get a chance to. My mom made me promise that if I rapped, I would have to keep my grades up, so I did just enough to keep her off my back. When people started seeing that what I was doing was profitable, school became an obstacle for them. I would have fools tell me that I would be making more money than the principal, so I should concentrate on my flows instead of school. It sounded cool, but I made a promise to my mother to finish school, and that was what I was gonna do. I'm not gonna say that I was an angel or anything. I would cut class to do songs—even at lunch time—anything I had to do to make it happen.

When I finished the record, I knew it was good, but I really didn't know what we had our hands on. I gave tapes to some cuddies, but I didn't know how people outside the turf would take to it. Because of Ray Luv single "Get Ya Money On," KMEL, the rap station in the Bay, gave us some love. I remember when I first heard my song "I Gotta Have It" on the radio. A DJ named Theo Nisahara, the most popular DJ at the time, played it. I was on Mark Ave with the cuddie from the crew, just smoking blunts and drinking forties, when a cuddie of mine told me they were playin' my song. I tell ya, I had an out-of-body experience. I couldn't believe that was me on the radio for the whole Bay to hear. The cuddies were so juiced that we hopped in the cars and rolled all around the turf, dancing and yelling, telling everybody who would listen that I was on the radio.

When we dropped the record that summer, I could feel something was about to happen. We had a strong street buzz, and slowly but surely, the record picked up momentum. It was a great time for Bay Area music then.

There were JT and the GLP, Dre Dog, Cougnut, and RBL getting down in Frisco; Dru Down, The Luniz, 3xCrazy, Richie Rich out in Oakland; Lil Ric in Richmond; and Brotha Lynch and CBo out in Sac. Man, I tell you, it was a good time to be a rapper.

When a little money came in, we got an office and a staff. Khayree's brother, Daraka, Rob Nonies, and a cat

MY OPINION

I knew from Vallejo named Mark came to work for us. They all were big parts of making Illegal Business happen.

The response from the streets let us know that "Sic Wit Dis" was a song everybody liked, so the decision was made to make a video. I wanted to do the video in the Crest, and that was the plan until the day came to film and the Vallejo Police Department shut me down. Since we didn't have the proper permits, they weren't trying to let us shoot a single scene, and they said if we did, they would take the cameras. That was fucked up!

I was able to get some fly shots from the top floor at a hotel in Emeryville, plus some shots at Khayree's house in Vallejo. All my cuddies from my crew that was on the streets were in the video, so I was satisfied with the final outcome.

Now, I got to keep it real and tell y'all that growing up, I was not lucky with the ladies. I was always the last one picked in sports and by chicks. See, I was the youngest of the boys in my family and the youngest in my crew, so the chassies weren't checking for me. I had a couple of girlfriends, but the girls weren't lining up to talk to me. When the CD came out, though, all that changed; girls who weeks before wouldn't even look my way were all of a sudden giving me rhythm.

Real talk! I took full advantage of the situation—full advantage! I made up for all the years of being shy and stuttering. If the girls were throwing it at me, I was catching like Jerry Rice.

Ray Luv came home from Quentin, signed to YBB, and got straight in the studio. It was cool having Ray back, 'cause I was going through a lot of shit that was new to me, and I could talk to Ray, 'cause he had been through it.

This is when Lathin Williams (a.k.a. Young Lay) came into the picture. Lay was from Lofas and was the younger cousin of Ray and Ronnie Waggs of the Romper Room Crew. He had just been released from juvenile hall, and the boy had heat. Ronnie Waggs introduced him to Khayree; Khayree heard him and quickly snatched him up.

Young Lay was the third artist signed to YBB I knew Young Lay before he went down. He was from North Vallejo, so we had seen each other around. He was a quiet cat, but once you got close to him, he was a comedian.

With Mac Dre in the feds, E40 became the king of Vallejo rap. If 40 was the king of Vallejo rap, then I was the prince. A lot of people don't know this, but 40 and I are cousins, with our roots goin' back to Louisiana. Actually, when I was younger, my mother and aunt wanted me to hook up with 40 and put out a record, since we were family. We chopped it up, but nothing ever came of it. It was at E40's "Practice Lookin' Hard" video that I met one of the hardest niggas to ever live, Tupac Amaru Shakur.

My cousin Shanda had brought me to the video; it was cool, even though I don't think I got in one scene. The thing that made it worth being there was when Pac showed up for his cameo. Pac was there with Mopreme, Stretch, Big Syke, and a couple of his folks from the Bay. He looked like success; at the time, he was on his way to becoming the biggest rap star alive, and the best thing about it was that he was from the Bay.

I remember back in the day when Pac ran with the Jungle, a turf in Marin. Mac Dre did a show out there, and our 'hoods had funk. We basically had to fight and shoot our way out of the projects, but that was then, and this was now. I can't front, I was star struck. I always related to Tupac, not only 'cause he was from the Bay but because I felt that when he rapped, he spoke for every young black man in America—shit, the world! He represented far you could take it if you worked hard and kept it real. Pac was at the video chillin' just like a regular person, only difference was that everybody was jockin' him. I remember he was smoking some chocolate ty he had brought back from New York.

My cousin Shanda, who was talking shit as usual, had made a remark about his weed, and that's when I took my chance to introduce myself. I walked up to him and said, "What's up, Pac? My name is Mac Mall." Then I gave him some dap.

When he heard my name, his eyes got big. Now, anybody who knew Pac knew how hyper he could get about shit. He was like, "You Mac Mall from Young Black Brotha? I love your shit, dog! Me and all my niggas is slammin' that shit right now! I know your manager, Leila. I'm gonna call you up; we got to do something!"

When I heard this coming out of the mouth of one of my rap idols and the biggest rapper in the game, I felt validated and honored. I finally felt like I was on the right track. Shit, if the best said I was good, then I had to be doing something right!

When he told me "we had to do something," I really didn't trip; in the rap game, when somebody tells you that, it's kind of like somebody in Hollywood telling you, "Hey, I'll call you, and we'll do lunch."

But Tupac wasn't Hollywood. He called Leila, whom he hadn't spoken to in a while, and the next time he was in the Bay, he came through the YBB studio to check out our operation and do some tracks with me and Khayree. It was during this visit that Tupac told us that he wanted to direct a video for a song on my record called "Ghetto Theme." I was floored! I couldn't believe he would take time out of his busy schedule to direct and be in a video for little ol' me. Tupac will forever be a friend in my eyes for that. Even now, I think about how God brought Pac into my life. I mean Tupac was large; he didn't even have to talk to me, let alone take me under his wing. I don't know why God did it, but I'm happy he did. Here I was in the eleventh grade with a CD in stores, doing shows around the country, starting to see a little paper, and having the biggest rapper as a big cuddie! It felt good; life was sweet!

But you can't have the sweet without the bitter. The bitter came in the form of hate; it seemed like the better I did, the more some people hated on me. It didn't bother me, 'cause I had my crew, but when some of them dudes started to hate, it really cut me deep. I had to come face to face with the fact that everybody wasn't going to see my dream the way I saw it. It hurt that rap came between us, but this was bigger than me. This was destiny I had to handle my business. Pac and I got close, and even though he was fighting cases, doing movies, and making music, I was still able to call him and ask him for advice or just to chop it up.

I remember when Pac wanted to take me to the Soul Train Awards that year. Since I was young, he decided he'd call my mom and ask her personally for permission rather than having his people do it. He couldn't have called at a worse time, 'cause I wasn't doing well in school. When he asked her, she straight up told him no. I almost fainted. I had to explain to her that this was a once-in-a-lifetime opportunity, and I had to get out there. Luckily I was able to get my grades together and go.

Man, going to Hollywood for the Soul Train Awards with Tupac was major! It also was the first time Ray Luv and Tupac had spoken since the Strictly Dope days. Strictly Dope was a group Pac and Ray started back in the day. Pac left the group to join Digital Underground, so he and Ray weren't on good terms. Once we hooked up with Pac, though, he and Ray went into a back room, chopped it up, and squashed whatever problem they had. When we got to the awards, I saw how the big dogs do it. It was superstars everywhere. Pac let me sit in the front next to him, while Ray and Thug Life had other seats in the back. Man, I was literally sitting next to Madonna, and Jamie Fox, Dr. Dre, and Snoop were by us.

Man, people I watched on TV were right in front of my face—not to mention, I was with the biggest rapper/actor in the game. "Man, if the cuddies could see me now," I thought.

After the awards, we went to a Death Row party and did it big! Dr. Dre was on the ones and twos; there were celebrities wall to wall.

Pac was in there being Pac and goin' wild, the party was packed, and I had the time of my life. I remember having to squeeze through the crowd and coming face to face with TLC.

Ray Luv always said that one of 'em was looking at me, but he never told me which one. Right then, I knew I wanted to step my game up and be on that level. Tupac was on!

What I didn't see was all the shit he had on his mind. It amazes me how he was able to keep it together and smile when he had the world on his shoulders. Tupac was so cool that he also agreed to do a video for Ray Luv's single "Last Night."

We shot both videos in LA. I had my mom out there, my cousin Shanda, the homegirl, Lynne, and a couple of cuddies from the turf. Ray Luv brought the Link Crew and some of his folks from Santa Rosa. Young Lay was there, plus JT the Bigga Figga.

Tupac was a godsend; this was the first time he had directed and was doing two videos in one day. He made the treatment, picked the film crew (Traci and Gobi, who shot all his videos and would later shoot most of mine), and basically ran the show. He was doing all this while he had cases in almost every state, but yet you could never tell by looking at him. He was upbeat and made everybody feel at home. My momma even had a good time. It was cool for her to meet him, because all she ever heard was people talking badly about him, and now she had a chance to see that he was a whole lot more than what they wrote about in magazines. Pac was a generous, caring, considerate, and beautiful person with a heart bigger than Texas. I know God brought us together for a reason. Once we had the videos, it was on and crackin'! A lot of new doors was open to me thanks to Pac.

Eventually I was able to keep my promise to my mom and graduate high school with the help of my homeboy Jay of the Romper Room Crew, who drove me to school every day in his clean root-beer-brown Camaro with hella beat!

Like he used to say, "Mac Mall is too cool to ride the bus."

Good lookin' for the wake-and-bake cuddie. Things at YBB were picking up, but what comes up must come down. Khayree was busy running the company, and I was busy being Mac Mall. This allowed people to get in my ears and try to split us up. I had fools telling me that Khayree was gonna rob me and that I'd better watch him. Together with the fact that I was getting big headed, this was a destructive combination.

Times were getting crazy, but we still got work done. I guess we all were feeling the pressure from outside, because we made the song "All about My Fedi." That song and video were special, 'cause it was the last time we were all together on YBB "All about My Fedi" got put on the soundtrack to the movie New Jersey Drive and was played all through the movie. We shot the video in the Bay, and it was hella fun. Young Lay was there with the Sic Set Crew, Ray was there with the Link Crew, some of the cuddies from the Crest were there, and DCon from the Romper Room Crew had just come home and was in the video.

Ricky Waters was there too. He was with the 49ers then and on his way to the Super Bowl. Ray hooked that up, since he was and still is a Niner fan. The video was boss; we flossed the Bay to the fullest and had a good time doing it.

Shortly after the "All about My Fedi" video, I was getting ready to leave YBB I'm not going to sit here and say that the reason I wanted to leave was that people were in my ear; I left for a couple of reasons. The main one was that when I got with Khayree, I was a little kid—raw talent. He basically led, and I followed. As time passed and I grew, I began to have a vision on where we should go with the music. No offense, but when it comes to music, Khayree is more like a dictator, and the only way to get a dictator to pay attention is to revolt.

I had a chance to go to Jack the Rappa, a rap convention in Orlando, with Ray Luv that year. It was mind blowing. I saw Suge Knight and Death Row in full force. I met Notorious B.I.G. and saw him perform.

I saw Puffy bossin' up, promoting with signs and a bullhorn and shit. The Bay was there; we kicked it with Too Short but spent most of our time with Yukmouth and Numb Skull of the Luniz. While we were parlaying, Yukmouth said a cat named AJ, who worked with CNote Records, had just hooked Dru Down up with Relativity Records and was interested in taking me up there and negotiating a deal for me. The thought of being on a major label had me open. I didn't know what it was all about; I just knew that I would have major money and push behind me, and I could get one thing I always wanted: control. Or so I thought. AJ was all business. I told him to make the call, and within a week, Leila and I were on a plane to New York to meet the heads of Relativity Records.

MY OPINION

My brother Ray Luv's first record, much love to him

My debut record

MY OPINION

2pac, Ray Luv and Me On the set of Ghetto Theme video

Khayree and 2pac with TJ in the back.

CHAPTER 3

THE PLANE TOUCHED down in New York City at 6:00 a.m. Leila, AJ, and I hopped in a limo, drove to Manhattan, and checked into a ritzy art-deco-style hotel called the Paramount.

Before we went to Relativity, we had a little mini meeting to discuss what Leila and I wanted out of the deal. This was the first time I saw how unprepared we were. It was cool, though, 'cause AJ was there, and he was more accustomed to dealing with the major, so he schooled us on the dos and don'ts. We got a better understanding of the situation, but we still didn't have a clue. I knew Illegal Business at the time had sold a little over two hundred thousand records, so I was aware we would have an advantage in the negotiations. AJ said he thought that we should call our own shots and that we should go for it! So we agreed on the amount for the budget and other issues concerning the contracts, hopped in the limo, and went to Relativity Records to make the deal.

Relativity was located in the middle of Manhattan. The whole operation represented professionalism. They had a fly office, A&R representation, and a staff of fifty to seventy-five people. Couriers were running in and out; I was really impressed. Relativity had signed Dru Down, Fat Joe, and Bone Thugs & Harmony, MC Ren, and a couple of other groups. You could say that they were up and coming; they were distributed by Red and had backing from Sony, which mean they had long capital bread.

Leila, AJ, and I met with the president, vice president, and president of promotions. When I first met them, I was shocked. I wasn't shocked because they were white; I was shocked because they were old—like in their mid- to late fifties. Just to think that these square senior citizens were making decisions in hip-hop threw me off a little bit. Anyway, we began to talk about business and money, and I began to warm up to the idea, because they sounded like they knew what they were doing.

When we began to discuss the budget, I basically told them what I wanted, and they gave it to me. They said yeah so fast that I wish I would've asked them for more. What I should've really done was holler at Fat Joe and CNote and see how their relationship with Relativity was. But they said yes to all my demands and had the dough, so I ran with them. Leila and AJ hooked up a great contract for me.

I had eighteen points, a six-figure budget that I controlled, and an imprint deal. We had an outline of the contract, but I didn't sign there. They would send the paper work to my lawyer, and he would give a once-over. If everything was cool, I would sign it, and everything would be done.

I guess Khayree found out I was in NYC, 'cause he was blowing Leila's cell phone up, trying to figure out what we were doing. It made me feel bad that we were doing this behind his back, but at the time, I felt this was my chance, and I had to do what I had to do.

New York was poppin'; I met KRS One, who was one of the most down-to-earth people I met in my life. I also got a chance to meet a dude who would have a big impact on me. His name was Tony Draper. Tone was the CEO of Suave House Records, Eight Ball, and MJG's label. He was in New York securing a deal with Relativity for Suave House. We met while he was having lunch with some of the suits from Relativity.

They introduced us, but I already knew about Suave House and MJG. Independent record labels are like small communities: if you're making moves, everybody knows. So he was also aware of YBB and what we were doing. We exchanged numbers, and he said we would hook up and do some business. I didn't know it then, but I would learn a lot from Tony Draper.

When I got back to the Bay, the cat was out of the bag. Khayree knew about the deal with Relativity, so we had a meeting and discussed the situation. It basically came down to me telling him what I was going to get at Relativity and asking if he could match it. He said he couldn't match it, and surprisingly, he gave me his blessing to sign to Relativity. That was cool of Khayree, 'cause he could have made it harder for me to sign.

Once my legal representation looked at the contract and OK'd it, it was official: I was signed to Relativity. I was more than juiced to start on my new record, and to finally have control musically was like being introduced to a world full of possibilities. The first thing I had to do was get a boss producer. I chose Mike Mosley, since I always liked him. He did music for E40 and CBo, and I knew if we hooked up, the outcome would be dope.

Mike Mosley is a real laid-back kind of person, so working with him went smoothly. The songs we did all came out hella vicious. Leila was making everything happen for me as far as doing the groundwork and making the calls to make my ideas become a reality. She hooked Mike up with a musician from Nigeria named Femi Ojtuneday, who became a key producer of Steady Mobbin Productions and a good friend and producer on almost every one of my records. Femi was a unique addition to my musical family; with him came Afro Cuban drums, Spanish guitars, and a whole lot of otherworld rhythms that we were never exposed to. Mike Mosley was putting together a tight team. Soon after, he recruited Ric Roc, a producer from Alabama who was really talented and brought something fresh to the table. We were ready to go. We did songs like "Straight Laced," "Get Right," and "Untouchable," which I decided was gonna be my title track. I guess I called it that 'cause the paper and position had me feeling that way.

Mike Mosley and Steady Mobbin Productions (Femi and Rick Rock) helped me construct and record my record. While doing "Untouchable," Mike introduced me to a rapper from LA named Young Dre. Young Dre and I had a lot in common; both being from turfs (him a Kitchen Crip and me a Crestsider), we represented to the fullest.

Both of us loved music; we quickly clicked, and he became a part of my family. While in LA, I got a call from Mike Mosley to come down to the studio and kick it with Tupac, Spice One, and Richie Rich. Young Lay was in LA with me, so we dropped what we were doing and went to the studio.

Mike Mosley was there producing a track for E40 that was to feature Richie Rich, Tupac, and Spice One. The studio was filled with smoke; anybody who knew Pac knew that he kept the blunts lit.

Anyway, after a couple of hours of kickin' it, Tupac looked at me and said, "Mall, why don't you take my eight bars and get on this song?" I was like, "Hell yeah, I wanna get on this song!"

Even though Spice and Rich knew me since I was like fourteen, and E40 was my blood relative, it took the biggest rapper in the world to give up his verse to get me on the track "Dusted and Disgusted." Like I said, Tupac was real; he always looked out for his people.

That's why I will always stay loyal to his legacy. E40 released the track on his CD In a Major Way and shot the video. Pac wasn't able to be there because he was locked up, but it still came out cool. It was a trip, 'cause I got a lot of shit from my turf for being on that song and video, but they had to understand that Pac game me a chance, so I took it.

I also took full advantage of having a big budget and worked with some producers that I was always a fan of, like Cold 187um from Above the Law. Going to LA and hooking up with Above the Law was dope. KMG (RIP), Cocaine, and Trigga Man are some real playas. That impressed me 'cause LA is all about gang bangin' and these dudes were no doubt some gangstas, but they also had much game.

The only bad thing about being out there was that three days after arriving to start recording with 187um, the world found out that legendary West Coast rapper Eazy E was dying of AIDS. It was a trip being out there and watching 187um and ATL go through all the drama that was poppin' off, but it also taught me about life, HIV and AIDS. The fact that Eazy (RIP) got it let me know that AIDS was real and was not something that only gays and drug addicts had to worry about, but it was something that everybody needed to acknowledge and protect themselves from.

Leila and I had to moved to Albany by then and I was hanging on Oakland with my dogg Reggie. I got introduced to Reg by my homeboy Jay of the Romper Room Crew. I also started recording with Tone Capone, who did "I Got 5 on It" for The Luniz and worked with 3xCrazy and Scarface. Tone was a boss; he always had the coolest working environment with some of the most potent weed I ever smoked. Tone worked with a producer named Harm and One Drop Scott.

Harm and Scott both became factors in Bay Area music.

They were both essential in making "Serving Game," the song I did with Tone Knock. I was able to hook up with the Bay Area rap pioneers Ant Banks and Too Short. I actually went to Atlanta, Georgia, and stayed with Banks in his big-ass house in the suburbs, about thirty minutes outside of Atlanta. Ant Banks was good people; not only did he let me live in his home for about a month, but he laced me on how to deal with major labels. Ant Banks was a comedian too; he kept me crackin' up, and he could make a hell of a mustard-fried chicken!

Too Short was, is, and always will be the man. I had known him for a while, but in the time I spent in Atlanta, I got to see a whole different side of Too Short: the family side. I met his mother, who is an educated woman and made some of the best gumbo I ever tasted. I also kicked it with his big brother, Wayne Loc, who I know Too Short got some of his coolness from. I also got to see the business side of Too Short: he was the CEO of Dangerous Music.

They had a big building with a big staff, fly offices, and a dope recording studio that I recorded *Untouchable* in.

Too Short's Dangerous Crew—dudes like P.O, Joc, and the rest of them—set it out for me. Those Oakland cats really had it on lock. Homeboy Jay from the Romper Room Crew came out there and kicked it with me, plus Ray Luv and Young Lay came out to record "Pimp or Die" for the Untouchable CD. While Ray and Lay were there, we got to go to a Players Ball that Too Short threw. We had hella fun out there—so much fun that Ray Luv wrecked the new Lexus we rented. It was crazy!

Between Mike Mosley, Femi, Ric Roc, Tone Capone, and Ant Banks, I had almost all of the production for my

CD. But what is a Mac Mall record without Khayree? So when I got back to the Bay, I made the call, and Khayree agreed to make a couple of tracks for me. Khayree had just signed a deal with Atlantic Records for big bread, so when we hooked up, we both had deals, we both had money, and we both had big egos. We didn't say anything, but in our heads, I know we both had something to prove to each other. Regardless of how we were acting, when Khayree and I do music, it's always dope, and the tracks we did for Untouchable were no different.

Before we wrapped up the record, I had an idea for the record cover. I knew that the record was called Untouchable, so I started to think of the most untouchable objects. Fire? Nah. What about a wild animal? What's the most untouchable wild animal?

A hyena? What about a lion? Then I had an epiphany: an alligator! I thought, "Yeah, you just can't go pet no alligator. Yeah, Ima have an alligator, and Ima clown on it!

Ima have an alligator on a chain like a pit bull!"

That was it. I had the album cover. When I told Ray, Leila, and Young Dre this shit, they thought I had smoked myself crazy, but as I explained it more, they felt where I was coming from. And once again, it was Leila to the rescue.

On this one trip she and Ray Luv took to New Orleans, they met a dude named Wild Will. Wild Will owned and ran an alligator farm in Louisiana. Leila, who was always shakin' hands, meeting friends, and on top of her business, got his number and kept it in her Rolodex. So Leila called Wild Will and made plans for me, my photographer Kathy, and her to go to Louisiana and get the shot for the cover.

A week later, we all got on the plane and flew to New Orleans, where we were supposed to meet Wild Will, who was coming back from Amsterdam the same day. When we got there, Wild Will wasn't there to meet us. He got caught up in customs trying to bring some hash back from Amsterdam. Right then, I should've known it was gonna be a crazy trip. After a couple of hours, they released him, and Leila made the introductions. We got our bags, met with Wild Will's sister, hopped in the van, and rolled to the gator farm.

We stopped once for gas and for Katy and Leila to get film. While they were in the store, I overheard Wild Will keep asking his sister for "the shit." First she said "no," but when Wild Will kept begging her, she handed him a eight ball of either cocaine or crystal meth. Wild Will asked me if I wanted some. I told him no, and then he snorted some of the powder and gave it back to his sister. When Leila and Kathy got back in the van, they knew something was up just by looking at me, but I didn't tell them what went down until later.

On the ride to the gator farm, which was located in a town called Thibodaux, Louisiana, about an hour outside from New Orleans, Wild Will decided to tell us about how back in the day, his town had a gate at the city limits to keep people out (but I think it was there to keep people in).

Then he told us about how in the fifties, some convicts escaped from the penitentiary, and the town was on full alert. A couple of days later, late at night, a black man went to a house, knocked on the door, and asked the white man who owned the house if he could have some water.

The white man told him to wait a minute, left, came back with a shotgun, and blasted the black man. If that wasn't bad enough, after they shot the brotha, they strapped him to the front of the truck and paraded him through town.

"What the fuck?" I thought. I came all this way, and the dude who was running the show was a racist dope fiend. Actually, I don't know if Will was racist; he was all right, but the story just tripped me out.

When we got to the alligator farm, it looked like The Dukes of Hazard but on a swamp. They had a big house where Will and his family lived, a houseboat right on the bayou, and a restaurant where they sold food, drinks, and pickaninny dolls. The pickaninny dolls pissed me off, but I chalked it up to ignorance. They were some inbred-lookin' mutha fuckas. Plus I had a job to do.

Leila, who was always trying to save money, suggested we stay on the houseboat. Once I saw what kind of condition the houseboat was in, I wasn't with it. Man, the houseboat was more like a shack boat.

There were wood floors, two beds with just some sheets on 'em, and was no running water. Wild Will gave me some weed and a couple of riffles just in case somebody fucked with us, but it was a no go.

Leila and Kathy were either soldiers or just crazy, 'cause they said they'd stay on the shack boat. I made Wild Will take me to the telly about thirty minutes away. The whole thing reminded me of a scene out of Deliverance, so I had to bounce.

The next day when I got to the gator farm, I got to see everything. I was trippin'; in the middle of their land, they had their own swamp, where they had all their alligators and all types of swamp wildlife, like snakes, turtles, and muskrats. And they had this one spot on the other side specifically for slaughtering gators; it was sick! Now straight up, I ain't no punk, but at that time, the only gators I saw were on the feet of preachers and pimps, so to see them alive, up close, and personal, I must admit that it had me shook. To make things worse, before I got there, Leila had an idea to shoot me in a pit with a couple of alligators of various sizes, so Wild Will and his crew were capturing gators and loading them into the pit. When they put two of the gators together, I guess the larger one wasn't feeling being out of the water, so he attacked the smaller gator.

The next thing they knew, they got locked in a death spin, which in nature is used to rip meat off their prey. The two gators locked jaws, hissed, and began to spin. The big gator must have twisted the wrong way, 'cause all of a sudden, all they heard was a big "Crack!" Man, the big gator tore the smaller one's jaw off!

If I'd been there for that, I never would have taken those pictures. I would have been on the next plane, smoking and headed back to the Bay. When I got there, I could see that Leila and Kathy were nervous, but I figured they just had a rough night. They told me bits and pieces, but I didn't know the whole story; I just knew the pit shot was canceled.

They started me off slow with baby gators, but I was still nervous; I didn't know what those little things could do. We got a couple of shots with them, and then we moved to a bigger female alligator. When I saw her, I was 'noid, 'cause she was hissin' hella loud. I ain't no dummy; I know that hissing meant she didn't want to be bothered and was about to take a chunk out of something.

I was shaky for a minute, but after about two rolls of film I began to loosen up—actually, I started to get mad at myself for being scared. It was hard trying to look cool with a wild animal in my hands that could kill or at least deform me with one bite, and I had Wild Will and his crew in my ear telling me with their country accents, "Grab that gator, Mall! You gotta show her who's boss!"

Yeah, it was a stressful situation, but Kathy was getting some tight shots. Everything was going as planned until the gator must have wanted to take a lunch break, because she whipped around and tried to take a bite out of me. The only thing that came into my mind was "run!" I wish my brain would have told my hands to drop the gator before it told my feet to run, because I know I carried that gator for three or four steps before I dropped her and ran off.

Once Kathy and Leila calmed me down, I was able to get the shot with me kneeling down holding the gator by the neck as well as the cover shot of me and the gator on the chain. All in all, the photo shoot was a success; even Wild Will and the people of Thibodaux turned out to be cool (but the pickaninny dolls were and are some bullshit).

Now that I had my cover and my record was finished, Leila sent the artwork to Relativity and me, and Mike Mosley and Rick Roc went to New York to master the record. One of Rick Roc's first beats ever on CD were on my intro; I would have rapped on it, but I had to turn the record in. Rick Roc went on to produce for Jay Z, Busta Rhymes, and his own group, the Federation. I chose "Get Right" as my first single; I thought it would be a good follow-up to "Ghetto Theme." I was cocked, locked, and ready to rock.

Professionally, I was beginning a new chapter in my life; personally, I was "feeling myself." Fools were still hating on me, but now I was giving them a reason to hate, because I stayed fly—out of a sucka way and all in a bad chick face! The Five Trey Five (which the crew was now known as) and I were livin'! Dubee had signed with Khayree, and Sleep Dank had signed with Rick Nelson and his new label.

I shot the video for "Get Right" in LA. Relativity and I disagreed on who should direct. I wanted to use Traci and Gobi, because they had shot "Ghetto Theme," but Relativity wanted to use some fool it had a working relationship with. After like a hundred phone conversations, they decided to let me work with both crews. Now, doing one video with two crews seemed like it would be easy, but having two crews made it harder than it should have been. I brought my family out there, my crew was out there, and Levitti was there to do his part on the hook. Shit, even Big Lurch, who had just moved to Vallejo two doors down from my momma's house, was there.

Leila's nephew, Charlie, had the starring role. I put all my folks who came to LA in the video. I even got Dubee's hair done in Shirley's so that he could be an angel in the video. Imagine that: Suga Wolf Pimp as an angel!

We went all through LA that night; we went to a ghetto-ass strip club, saw a dead body, and got kicked out of our telly. "See, it really don't matter where we at, some Crest macks gonna be at that!"

Everybody enjoyed themselves in LA, and the video came out saucy. The only problem was when it was time to edit. Relativity chose its director to edit the video, and even though I wrote the treatment to this sort of "Ghetto Theme Pt 2" the director edited the video, and it had nothing to do with the "Ghetto Theme" story line. I basically had to go to the studio and edit the video myself! Relativity wasn't feeling my "take charge" attitude, and this would be the start of a power struggle that lasted my whole time at Relo, but at the end of the day, I got what I wanted. What started out as my vision ended up being my video.

We dropped the video, dropped the album, and hit the road. Ceese and I did a promotion tour and traveled all over the United States. The Bay was on lock, but I wanted world domination. I definitely saw the difference of being on a major compared with being on an independent label. On a major, you don't have to worry about the same problems you have to worry about on an independent label, but there are other problems. Mine was trying to make an independent style fit in the corporate frame of a major label.

I wasn't trippin' then, though, 'cause it was all gravy. I was on Rap City with Big Lez and all in the magazines; I even got a few covers. Since Dru Down and I were on the same label, we did a lot of shows together. One time when we were in LA doing a Dru Down Pimp of the Year party, Young Dre, Reg from Oakland, and I saw Halle Berry in the mall. We tried to get her to come to the show, and she was with it until some fools working in the mall sweated her for an autograph and ran her off. Shit, we still talk about that to this day.

I liked doing shows with Dru Down, because he brought Oakland with him. When we both brought our folks, the Bay would be in the building thick! My record was doing well; we had sold a couple a hundred thousand, and I was feeling that if I dropped another single, I could snatch a gold plaque.

The suits at Relativity and I weren't seeing eye to eye on this situation. See, on an independent label you work a record as long as it takes, but on a major, if the first single doesn't fly, then they want to start a new record. Leila and I basically had to strong-arm those fools to do a video for my second single, "Let's Get a Telly."

I shot the video in Frisco at a bed and breakfast near Fillmore. The 535 Crew was there, and Mac Dre (who had just came home from the feds) was there along with OG DCon (who had just come home from a murder beef). I also was able to get a fly female emcee that I was messin' with from LA to get in the video and play my girl. JT, the Bigga Figga, was there, and I had my cuddie Jabar from the turf in a couple of scenes. I also bought my first pair of Mauri gators and flossed them like Tony Draper in the video.

The video came out dope; it was colorful and funny, but by the time we dropped the video, my relationship with Relativity was almost at the boiling point. I guess they wanted me to be a good little slave and do as I was told, but I was too street to conform to a corporate suit. One time when I felt one of the suits was trying to get smart with me, I told him I was going to bust his fuckin' head! So as you can probably tell, it didn't take long for the line of communications to come to a complete close.

But I wasn't trippin' 'cause having the senior citizens at Relo over my head were driving me crazy. I didn't have a problem with doing my thing at an independent, so I was trying to get my walking papers and bounce, but the suits had a different plan, and the plan was to starve me out.

They sicced the corporate lawyers on me and wouldn't let me out of my contract, and since I was signed to them, they wouldn't clear me to do features with other artists.

That made it almost impossible for me to make money. If it wasn't for shows, it would have been uglier than it was. I got to say this was one of the hardest times in my life. Like I said, hip-hop was my heart, and these fools was trying to make my heart stop. But man, I was a soldier, a fighter. I wasn't about to let Relativity or anybody stop me from doing my thing; I'm from the do-or-die Crestside, bad times ain't never made us hide it—only made us ride!

I got a lot of work done that year in spite of me being in litigation with Relativity. I said fuck it. The lawyers could see me in the street and the cuddies from the Romper Room and I did the Rompalation. JT the Bigga Figga and I wrote, funded, and starred in our own movie called Beware of Those. It made me feel strong to carry on through adversity, but I was fiending to make a new record. I know God must have felt me, 'cause he put an old friend back in my life to make prayers come true. That friend's name was Khayree.

Me, Young Lay and Ray Luv at the Player's Ball in Atlanta

Me, Mike Mosely, DJ Yon

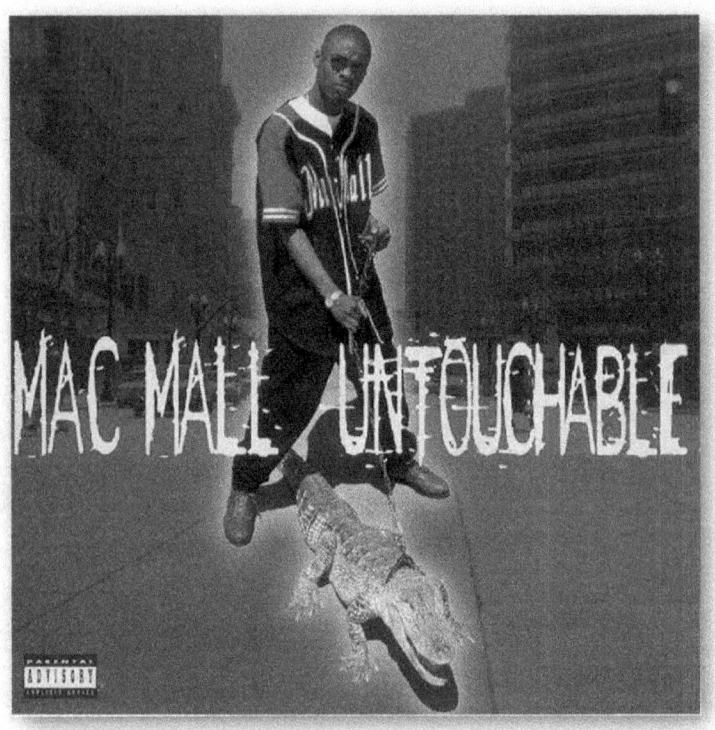

My second album Untouchable.

MY OPINION

Untouchable photo shoot, Mac'n with my hands around the gator neck.

Promo pic from Relativity Records

CHAPTER 4

I wasn't alone when I was going through the shit with Relativity; Leila was right there with me. It was hard on both of us, and it put a lot of unneeded stress on our relationship. See, Leila had a different kind of stress: she was a mother with three kids and one on the way. You could say she had four and one on the way, 'cause she took care of me like a mother does a son, but she couldn't protect me from the hardships of going back and forth to court with Relativity. Besides the Rompalation, I wasn't recording any more new music, and with the lawyer fees and living expenses, my money was getting funnier than Mike Epps. Around that time, I was kicking it tough with my boy Reese, who I like to call Reese the Beast. Reese was an Oakland triple OG and the definition of a gangsta mack—the type of cat who been through it all, from turf wars to penitentiary walls, and had shaken it off and still remained hard.

Reese reminded me of my Uncle Mike, who was in the feds for bank robbery. We would smoke back-wood blunts and chop up every angle of "the Game." One of the angles that sparked my interest was pimpin'. Being from the Crestside, I was born to mack.

Some people who are less educated in the Game might think a mack and a pimp are the same, but the two are totally different. A pimp's specialty is controlling a female, and he gets all the paper from a chick. Like they say, if a chick doesn't pay, then a pimp doesn't eat. I mean, a real pimp won't even think about selling dope, where as a mack is not just one thing; a mack masters every aspect of the Game. Give a mack a strap, and he knows how to react; give a mack a sac, and he knows what to do with that. You could put a mack in the 'hood or the Hamptons, and he could make it happen.

I guess since I was a control freak, the pimp game sounded sweet to me. Not saying that the money wasn't a factor, 'cause I was needing loot, but control is like a drug for me—a drug that's almost impossible to kick.

Another thing that kind of drove me to pimpin' was my relationship with women. Like every male, when I was younger, I had my heart broken and was pretty much ignored by girls, but when I started rappin', it was different. Females were paying attention, and I took full advantage by personally trying to fuck every bad broad that got by me. I was sort of using sex as a way to control women, which didn't last long, 'cause I soon found that just because it's with you they lay doesn't mean it's you they obey. Most of the broads I was dealing with had boyfriends, husbands, baby daddies, or at least a stalker or three. They would fuck me porno style, but if I had a cold and needed a bowl of chicken soup, they were nowhere to be found.

When it came to the music business, there wasn't much activity. I recorded the Rompalation with Mac Dre and DCon, but I didn't see much mail from that. I pretty much had my back against the wall.

I had some personal tragedies happen to me at this time too. My grandmother, Juanita Rocker, and my grandfather, Catez Davis, died two weeks apart, and my DJ and mentor, DJ Ceece, got murdered in the Crest. Also Young Lay's baby momma, Daphney, who I grew up with, was killed, and their baby was kidnapped, so it was a really dark time for me.

I can't front; I thought I was gonna go crazy. The thought of having a female down for me and getting it by any means necessary seemed attractive to me. It didn't take long for me to be introduced to the first broad who would be on my team. She was a fly Asian chick who was a savage about money. She was about five foot four with blond hair, a nice ass, and a tattoo that said "daddy's little bitch." It didn't take long for us to click and for her to choose on me quickly.

There was only one problem: she belonged to an Oakland pimp who was supposed to be big shit. But no man can get in the way of my money, so I served him the news. For those who don't know, that means I called him and told him that his woman belonged to me. Then it became official: Mac Mall the rapper became Mac Mall the rapper/pimp.

Khayree, who like I said was a genius, made sure that every time I went to the studio, we recorded extra songs so that he was able to stockpile more than a album's worth of material. He came up with an idea to revamp the music, and since it was recorded in the Illegal Business/Untouchable sessions, we decided to call it Illegal Business 2000. It felt good to be back in the saddle and ride with Khayree again; this time, though, we would be partners, splitting everything down the middle. He even upped the ante by giving me 50 percent ownership of the original Illegal Business. He and J. King were the first ones to lace me about how owning your masters was the key to controlling your destiny in this music business. Things were coming together for me, which was cool, 'cause the whole Relativity shit had me not really feeling music. But like MC Ren said, "If it ain't rough, it ain't me."

Not soon after I started Illegal Business 2000, Mac Dre, who was like my big brother, and I fell all the way out. It's not my style to put family business in the street for the public to peep, so I'll just say that one day we almost came to blows over something stupid. The next thing I knew, cuddie had a song about me. I'll admit it fucked me up, mainly 'cause my dude was kinfolk. How could he be callin' foul when all I ever did was hold him down? It was messed up, but Big Ern, a Crest OG, told me, "Keep it in a Mac fashion." So I stayed in the lab and on my path.

One day at the studio, Khayree was working on a song he wanted me to do called "Wide Open." At first, I didn't want to put the song out, 'cause it was so different from anything we ever did, but Khayree saw something I didn't see and basically made me put it on the record, and I'm glad he did.

While I was making Illegal Business 2000, I got a call from my big cuddie Ant Banks, who had moved back to the Bay from Atlanta, to come through and drop a verse for Boo from the Dangerous Crew artist Dolla Will. I went up there and laid the verse and was gonna bounce until Banks asked me if I wanted to lay a verse on a song he, Rappin' 4-tay, Captain SavaHoe, and Too Short had did called "Playas Holiday." I did the verse, went home, and never really thought anything of it until Ant Banks formed the group TWDY (The Whole Damn Yay) with 4-tay and Captain and signed to Thump Records.

The next thing I knew, we were in LA shootin' the video. The video for "Playas Holiday" was off the chain!

Bay Area bosses on the yacht in the marina, drunk as fuck with a bunch of models. A good time was had by all. While I was out there, I really got a chance to check things out, and I thought that if I had a chance, I would like to live out there one day.

"Playas Holiday" blew up; the video got play on BET and MTV. We toured all through the United States, and I even got to do Soul Train! That was icing on the cake, and the cherry on top, man, was just being in the studio and meeting Don Cornelius. That was like a dream—I mean, a lil nigga from the Crest going from Sawyer Street to Soul Train. Dig that!

Being down with Banks and TWDY definitely helped me with the release of Illegal Business 2000 and "Wide Open." KMEL slowly started playing me, since I already had a song on the airwaves, and when the females from the Yay got down with the song, it straight blew up, which in turn made the record sell like hot cakes.

Jay King of the Timex Social Club, who always played an advisor roll in my career, made it possible for me to shoot a video for "Wide Open" and also hooked me up with a beautiful young woman from Oakland to star as my girl in the video. I wanted to have a sista who looked more like an "around the way" girl rather than the average video chick. Baby girl and I looked good together; she was perfect, and the video came out dope.

Jay also hooked me up with an independent publicity firm named XXposure, located in New York, that was ran by a cool-ass cat named Angelo Eleby. At the time, they worked with DMX, Eve, Mary J. Blige and even Dion Warrack. I would go to New York, and they would have me doing like fifty interviews a day.

On one of the trips to New York, Angelo hooked me up with a listening party for the press. He even hooked up one of my favorite MCs, Big Daddy Kane, and his DJ, Clark Kent, to host. Meeting Big Daddy Kane and him actually knowing who I was was unbelievable. He was one of the reasons I chose to spit game—I was fa sho juiced! Angelo also set up an event that would change my life. He hooked it up for me to do a show at the world-famous Apollo Theater, located in the mecca for blacks all over the United States: Harlem.

On the day of the performance, we rode the subway to the theatre. The whole way up there, I was shook, but when we go to the Apollo Theater, the security guard recognized me and gave me props on the verses I spit on "Playas Holiday," that made me loosen up.

I figured if homeboy dug my flow, then I should be able to rock the average New Yorker. There's only one word that best describes the Apollo: historic. Since 1934 the Apollo has made or slayed the dreams of many black performers. Everybody that was anybody rubbed that log, stepped on that stage, and gave his or her all—

everybody from Ella Fitzgerald to Billy Holiday to James Brown to Michael Jackson and now, Mac Mall. I could hardly sit still. Later that night when it came time for me to perform, I was a ball of nerves. You couldn't tell by lookin' at it on TV, but the Apollo is small. The audience is so close to the stage, it's almost like the audience is on top of you. So DJ Yon, who was my new DJ now, started the show, and it was on. I stepped onstage; I rubbed the log and pimp walked into my first song.

I couldn't see the crowd 'cause of the stage lights, but the people I did see were bobbin' their heads and rockin', so I was cool. When "Playas Holiday" came on, they got hype, and I had them where I wanted them.

I didn't know it then, but while we were performing, DJ Yon had his eye on the Sandman, a clown the Apollo used to usher the people who got booed off the stage. Yon saw the Sandman dancing to our music and didn't know whether he was loving us or about to sweep us off the stage. It turned out he was feeling us, so everything was everything. My night at the Apollo was a success.

Something crazy happened when I was in New York. While reading the Source Magazine, I read that Loud Records had bought Relativity, and with the purchase of Relativity, it also bought the labels roster that I was on. This put me in an awkward position.

I could ignore them and keep doing my thing guerrilla style or take a second chance on a major and make a deal. I decided to make a deal.

My manager Leila Steinburg and Nikko.

My third record Illegal Business 2000

MY OPINION

Me in New York at the Apollo before I did the showcase.

Me rubbing the famous log at the Apollo before I went on stage.

MY OPINION

Me at the Wide Open video shoot with my lovely co-star.

CHAPTER 5

Loud Records was an underground, friendly, rap label that bought Relativity and had offices in New York and LA. I felt comfortable about signing with them, 'cause they had artists like Wu Tang Clan, Xzibit, and the Alkaholiks. It seemed like they really got behind their artists and concentrated on the craft and not the cash; it was cool.

Leila was already living back in LA, and she hooked up the deal. I got my eighteen-point imprint deal and the same budget. The only problem was that I didn't have control of it. I got a cool advance, and we had a say on where we spent it, but they wrote the checks. Back in the Bay, I was doin' it, movin' with no breaks. Like I said, I had knocked the fly, fast-ass Asian chick who was a money magnet. We both grew up poor and were young and hungry, so it was all good. When I started getting money from rap and the track, there was no looking back.

Some pimps didn't like the fact that I was in the Game, but my people Reese the Beast and OGs like CNote from Richmond and Gangsta Brown from Oakland had my back, so I wasn't trippin'. Letting somebody stop me from getting money wasn't my style. I followed all the old-school pimp rules, so dudes had to accept and respect it.

They got an old saying I once heard: "Money won is better than money earned." For me, that couldn't be more real. You couldn't tell me anything! Leila and I were starting to slowly drift apart. Leila was all about women's liberation, education, and spiritual salvation, while I was dealing in degradation and receiving compensation from a pimp situation, so we were definitely on two different pages. The drama I went through with Relativity (as far as not being able to record or make money) had me on some rather-die-than-be-broke shit. No way was I gonna let a record company have me broke, so I kept one foot planted in the Game.

Like I said, the first broad on my team was a go-getter. She also was bisexual, so it didn't take me too long to get too deep with no sleep (meaning I had two girls). My main chick brought home a young, black, red-bone slim goody who was green to the game but up for learning. She had the choosing fee, so I let her be down.

I decided I should move to LA to be closer to Loud and business in general. Since I left my momma's house, I always had a fly pad. Whether it was in Albany in the condo on the thirteenth floor with a panoramic view of San Francisco or my spot in the skyscraper in Emeryville, I did it lavish. So when I moved to LA, I wasn't going to move to the Valley; I was going to be in the middle of it. I found a dope two-bedroom loft on Beverly Boulevard right next to the CBS building. Afani Shakur, Tupac's mom, helped me get in the building, and I actually got to stay in the loft that Pac once owned; it was hella cool. There you had it: the Bay Area boss takes the game to La-La Land.

Southern California and Northern California are like night and day. Don't get it twisted; it's all killa Cali, but in my opinion, Los Angeles has two sides: Hollywood and the 'hood. But when it comes to the music business, the rap music business, even Hollywood is secretly run by the gangs in LA. You can't be running around the streets and not be clicked up with some Crips or riding around with some powerful Bloods.

That's why you see rap cats from all around the country move to LA and within a year be like, "What's up, cuz!

What's up, blood!"

Best believe that when your favorite rapper comes to LA to do shows, he or she is paying a gangbanger for protection. Luckily my playa patna Yorel, who was from Southern California but lived in the Crestside, had moved back to LA and was doing it big. When I got there, he introduced me to his cousin Steele, his brother Kenyata, and his homeboy CBop, who was down with sixties Crip. CBop is a hoodsta through and through, but he was also boss business minded. I thought it was cool that he, the rest of the LA cats, and I became folks for real. CBop had a custom leather jacket and a clothing store on Crenshaw. I would spend a lot of time there or next door getting my hair cut by Kenyata at the barbershop. Some of the only rappers that I considered friends were the Alkoholiks (J. Roe, Tash, E. Swift, and my nigga Phil the Agony). Those dudes took it upon themselves to make sure my transition from the Bay to LA went smooth.

They made sure I was at the right parties and got introduced to the right people. Between Yorel and CBop and the 'liks, I was Hollywood swingin'! Loud Records hooked me up with two young A&R reps: one was named Shane Mooney, and he who was the son of legendary Black comedian Paul Mooney; and the other was named Malik Leavey, who was originally from Richmond, California. These cats were helping me find producers for my Loud release.

They introduced me to Battle Cat, Meech Wells and other well-known LA producers. I was ready to put together some heat. LA is wild; the most beautiful women from all across the world come to LA to be discovered or to discover an entertainer or an athlete who will take care of them. I lived a couple of blocks from Sunset Boulevard, so I stayed partying. We partied at Miyagi's, Dublins, 360, and the Good Bar. Yorel and I were tearin' up the clubs Bay Area style, havin' big fun!

Game wise, all was lovely. My ministable was happy, money was being made, and I had fooled myself into believing that I could balance the streets and the industry. You couldn't tell me anything; I couldn't be saved by John the Pope, Louise Farrakhan, or Jesse mutha fuckin' Jackson! Looking back, I think I could have handled my business a little different, like I shouldn't have had both breezies living with me. A square would think having two broads in the same building, sometimes in the same bed, would be a dream. It had its perks, but one thing you must know is that women hate other women, girlfriends hate girlfriends, sisters hate sisters—shit, sometimes daughters hate mothers, or vice versa. I stayed squashing beef between the two; they fought like Rodan and Mothra, so I would have to remind them that I was Godzilla yada mean!

Living in Hollywood was crazy, 'cause you would see TV and movie stars everywhere, like Whoopi Goldberg riding down Beverly in her green drop bug or Ice T at the club chillin' solo like a boss. Shit, I would even see Andy Dick at the park looking hella funny. I got a kick out of seeing all the celebrities, but the overall Hollywood attitude got played out quickly. Man, my weed man out there once told me he couldn't serve me 'cause he was at lunch—imagine that!

The little balancing act that I was trying to maintain with my street life and my square biz was starting to get to me. I was being a rapper in LA and running bitches in the Bay—basically spreading myself way thin. I stayed calling Reese the Beast and CNote for advice. They both would lace me up tight, and I would be straight, but honestly, when I concentrated on one, the other suffered.

Leila knew I was turning to the dark side, but she was still trying to hold it together. She got tracks together for me to work on from Khayree and Young Lord, a producer who was down with Bad Boy. I was recording with Femi, who had moved to LA, and we had Studio 56 on Santa Monica Boulevard as our home base. I knew that this was a big opportunity, so I wanted to make the dopest record possible. The staff at Loud seemed hyped about my project, and with their support, I was sure that I could be a factor in West Coast hip-hop.

I'm not exactly sure when it started, but Loud Records began to have problems, and the company laid off a lot of people in its New York office and fired 75 percent of its LA office. All the people who were excited about my record had lost their jobs. Even Malik, the A&R from Richmond, got fired. But Shane Mooney was still there, so we kept moving on the record.

I came up with the idea of pairing myself with a pop R&B female and doing a song like "Wide Open" to the tenth power. We threw a couple of names around, but I was trying to holla at Mya; I thought we would be dope together. So Leila had some of her people holla at Mya's people, and the deal was almost done until Loud started slackin'.

I guess Loud Records was losing major paper, and Sony began to step in and downsize the company. My team and I were trying to get a monster single together, but it was becoming difficult to get in contact with the head honchos over at Loud.

After about a week, Leila and I got in contact with Steve Rifkin, the president at Loud. I gotta say, he kept it real. He let us know that Loud was going through big changes, and he wanted me to stay down, but they would have to put my project release date back like nine months. I wasn't with that; being from the Bay, I was born with that independent attitude, so I hollered at him about getting my masters and doing my own thing. He was cool with the idea, but he wanted me to give him some loot when the record started selling. No problem. Steve Rifkin basically gave me the ownership to two records' worth of material. I would be able to really kick off my own label, Sessed Out Records, using the music I recorded with Loud. I had a positive outlook on releasing a record on my own label. My Illegal Business 2000 record was released on YBB/Sessed Out Records, and "Untouchable" was put out on Relativity. I had an imprint deal with them (meaning my logo got put on the record), but I really didn't have the juice you have as partners with the label. Being in this position made me excited: the world was full of possibilities.

Rob Noniz, who used to work for Khayree at YBB, had gotten a prime position with a distribution company called Bay Side, which was owned by Russ Soloman. He also owned the Tower Music chains around the company and wanted to get into the distribution game. He hired Rob Nonies and a cat named B12. They were signing and cashing out everybody. They got JT the Bigga Figga, MC Eight, Booya Tribe, and the Outlawz. Since I had a prior relationship with Rob Noniz, and Bay Side had the bread, Leila hooked up the deal, and I started working on a new record.

Like I told you before, I was wild trying to balance mackin' and rappin'.

While I would be focusing on one, the other would be falling apart. Now it wasn't this simple but I would just say I was going through playa stress. I went from two hoes to one hoe and then from one hoe to zero. I admit, blowing my main chick fucked me all the way up but I just threw myself into the music. I got cashed out by Bay Side, opened up an office on Pico Boulevard, and opened up shop. Since I was already working on a record, all I had to was touch up a couple of the songs and do some new songs. Then I would have a complete CD. Femi helped me finish up the songs and do new ones. We recorded most of the new songs at QD3, Quincy Jones's son's studio. When I was done, I decided to call the record Immaculate, since I felt like it was flawless.

Personally, I was doing fine about two or three months out of the Game when temptation kicked down my door once again. Temptation came in the form of a Canadian broad I had hollered at when I was in Canada with Tone Capone doing some music for a dude named Fast J (RIP) and Vic Voka. She was tall, thick Armenian chick who was a pro but also a groupie. When we first kicked it, I actually dissed her, 'cause she tried to fuck me without choosing up and payin' a pimp. When I met her the first time, I was still two deep, running full steam ahead, so when she tried to free fuck me, I told her to kick rocks.

Anyway, it was weird how when I got out of the Game and was rapped out, she decided to shake a Jamaican she was with and track me down. She went on the Internet, found YBB's website, and left an email saying it would be financially in my benefit if I called her. When I got the word, I couldn't help but get in contact with her. I gave her a call, we chopped it up, and when she came to LA, we met again face to face.

She really wasn't my type, but in the Game, I figured I didn't want to deal with a chick I actually liked. I learned that from my first broad. Since we were so much alike, and she was the first female I shared my life with, I'll admit that I caught feelings. This time it wasn't gonna be like that; I was gonna prove that me getting in the pimp game was no fluke. I told the chick she could be down, but she would have to give me a proper choosing fee. Now, the most I ever got from one of my broads back then at one time was $10,000, so I told her she would have to bring me a $20,000 choosing fee to get down with my program. See, I figured if I was gonna go out, then I was gonna go out mackin'. Either she was gonna pay the fee to see, or she was gonna get away from me.

Surprisingly, she told me that she could handle that. She went back to Canada for a week or two then went straight to Las Vegas, where she knew people and got down before. Real talk, it took her about 2 1/2 trips to have my money together, but when she did, I was back in the Game with a vengeance.

My fourth album Immaculate, one of my favorite records

CHAPTER 6

Life is about choices and consequences. The smallest thing you do could have the biggest consequence. At this point in my life, I wasn't concerned with consequences; I was concentrating on my cash. I wanted to have my cake and eat it too. Returning to the Game wasn't an easy decision for me to make, even though I made the decision with my balls more than my brains. My ego made me live on the edge, and my ambition pushed me over. I had some new work, and I was introduced to a new place to get paper: Las Vegas, Nevada. When I first got in the game in the Bay, I figured that I would learn the rules in the concrete jungle and then run my game in the neon jungle.

Since my new broad was already getting down out there, I figured this time was better than never. Las Vegas is the city of big money and broken dreams. Lights shine bright enough to see from space, but the underworld is as dirty as a devil's asshole. The City of Sin was just my speed: a twenty-four-hour party town with a plethora of pros for a pimp coach to draft on his team. I could dig that. The first thing I noticed about Vegas was that out there, the rules were different.

True, Las Vegas' game is played for high stakes at a fast pace, but the rules are not strictly enforced like they are in the Bay. Shit that would get you merked or at least run off the set was standard practice in Las Vegas. But it didn't take long for me to learn the lay of the land and start putting it down in LV. Back in LA, Leila and the Sessed Out Records staff were preparing for Immaculate to drop.

They threw me a record release party on Sunset Boulevard at Club 360. At first I didn't like how Leila planned the party without me, but once I got there, the party was fly. Ray Luv was there, cuddie Reese the Beast was there, and my patna Yorel was there flossin' and poppin' a million bottles of Crystal.

C-Note from Richmond was there bossin' up in the building, and a host of players, squares, and Hollywood types were in attendance. Yeah, I was impressed with the party; it was a proper way to set off the release of Immaculate.

The record came out, and it was back to business. But something was going wrong, because although the record was moving at the Tower chain stores, the mom-and-pop stores and other competing chains and distribution companies were not getting their orders on time, which affected my sales. I felt that it was Leila's responsibility to keep the pressure on Bay side and make sure our product was available to buy. We both had a lot riding on this, so things at the office stayed tense.

When it got weird in LA, I would shoot to Vegas and handle illegal business. My Canadian chick was highly enthused to get my loot, and I was checkin' paper, but as I spent more time with the broad, I started to see that she was game goofy, hella bootsie, and straight-up loony. I would lace her up like Timberland boots with that good game but end up having to explain to her like she was a slow student fresh off the short bus. She was as stubborn as a mule, which made me adjust my tactics to suit the situation. I had to get more gorilla than King Kong and Mighty Joe Young.

Pimpin' ain't easy, but I was up for the job. The more money I touched, the harder I would mack.

Poor Leila. All she could do was sit there and watch helplessly as I became immersed in the Game. Even if she had tried to voice her concerns, it wouldn't have mattered, 'cause I was too far gone. You couldn't have told me anything! Leila got an A for effort, but we were just livin' in two different worlds. It was hard for us to communicate without arguing, so in my head, it went from being Leila and I against the system to Leila and the system against me.

This was strange, 'cause we had always been close like brother and sister, mother and son but like I said before, people handle stress differently. The stress of dealing with Bay Side and their unprofessional business practices had me mackin' the most, playing the streets close, and I guess the stress of dealing with me made Leila retreat to her first love, which was teaching. She began to hold classes at the Pico office for poets, singers, rappers, and other artists. This didn't sit well with me, 'cause I was used to having her all to myself.

Leila always did other little side projects, but this time, I felt in a way that she was abandoning me for the class. To me, it pushed us further apart.

Immaculate did well as far as independent standards go, but I was expecting more.

When it wasn't my biggest-selling record, I was disappointed. I took Immaculate as a failure, even though it sold more than most independent records sell on their best day.

On the flip side of the coin that was my life, Vegas was becoming a second home. Out there, I was introduced to a cast of high rollers, sac holders, street soldiers, boss macks, and pimp posers. Ice-cold money-making hoes and backward bum bitches, wide eyed with runny noses. Con men, card sharks, drunks, junkies, shot callers, flunkies, CEOs, Mafioso's, gang bangers, game haters, and suckas of every age, ethnicity, size, walk of life, and color came to Vegas by the planeload to get drunk, get fucked, and get broke. The casinos weren't the only ones to profit from the vices of the tourists; all the locals got their loot too.

Existing in excess was a life that agreed with me. I stayed on my money mission, but I'd be lying if I said I wasn't out there drinking, drugging, funning, and stunting. I wasn't thinking about rappin'; I was distracted by mackin' and stackin' for a mansion. I didn't even watch videos back then. I would turn the channel and say something like, "Them fools is hella square!" I let the disappointment of Immaculate plus the bad, bad blood between me and Leila push me deeper and deeper into the dark side.

At the time, I was spending more time in Vegas than in LA. I was living the fast life, dancing on the edge. I was a stray being led but never really cared for. Cash was king, and the game was good to me. Little mama was doing it movin'. She would try to test me, and I would pass with flying colors, every time quick to put my mack hand down and keep her in line. I know y'all might wonder if I was feeling bad while I was out there doing my thing. To tell the truth, nah, I didn't feel anything. One of the key things you must possess to even exist in The

Game is the ability to turn your feelings off like a light switch, sort of like a machine—action without emotion.

Since I was in Las Vegas more than Los Angeles, I decided I should shake my spot in LA and move to my spot in Vegas. I told myself then that I was going out there to maintain my game, but what I was really doing was running away from my destiny, evading my fate. What I should have done was gone back to the lab, revamp my craft, and come back out like a sav, but hindsight is twenty-twenty, and money had me blind to the fact. Me moving to Vegas played right into the chick's hands. She was insecure when it came to my rappin', feeling like the more success I had with my career, the less I would need her, so she didn't support me at all.

I'm not saying that I needed her to push me, but if she wasn't with me, she was against me. Now that LV was my HQ, I was alone to do wrong. I dove deeper into the drinks and drugs, mackin' hard with no regard. I was waking up every day and, like I heard Ice T say, "Putting one foot to the ground and the other in a chicks ass." I could see now that I used drinking and drugs to numb myself to the reality of me not doing what I was meant to do: being Mac Mall, rapper extraordinaire and CEO of Sessed Out Records.

Instead I was just Mac Mall the pimp. But at the time, being Mac Mall the pimp was fine with me.

MY OPINION

I fell in love with the lights, camera, mackin' aspect of Sin City. I was cool with the whole cast of American Pimp, from shot callers at casinos to hosts at high-class restaurants. **Maître d's** gave me love because I tipped big. I found that a big tip would get you the keys to the city in Las Vegas. I was cool with boxers like Diego Corrales (RIP), who was from Sacramento and a soldier in the ring, and the champ Money Floyd Mayweather, who would be all around Vegas stuntin' in a fleet of foreign cars for sure! Yeah, I was feeling it. I didn't just want my name in the big Game book; I wanted my own chapter—fuck it, my own volume! Man, I was so on one that I didn't even know if I would make another record. Leila hadn't given up on me, though. She secured a deal with my first distribution company, City Hall.

City Hall had put out Illegal Business, Illegal Business 2000, and Mallenium, so we always had a good relationship. Now, I was never dumb, but I've always been hard headed. I made myself believe that I could play the game and do my thang. Maybe it was the Gemini in me—you know, the dual sides of my mentality—that had me thinking that I could achieve it all. So Mac Mall the pimp got back in the studio to do what once defined him and create a dope rap record.

Leila hooked up Studio 56 in LA for me to record when I wasn't in Vegas getting paper. It was a hard process, 'cause I was half assin', so of course, I was having problems. Recording was made more complicated, because Leila and I weren't communicating at all. If we did, it would be through a third person. She came to the studio a couple of times to make sure everything was moving along, but we wouldn't say more than a sentence to each other. It was sad.

Every record I'd ever done reflected the time and the mind state I was in; this CD would be no different. My subject matter—even the music I selected—reflected the depth of my involvement in the Game; I'm talking about pimp shit to the next level!

Femi held me down with the production, along with H2O, who actually worked with Sessed Out and was a key component in the making of the record. I also worked with a talented-ass cat from Fresno named Yaku. Tone Capone gave me a track, and a new producer named Izm gave me a tight beat.

Around this time, my cuddie Jamal Diggs was released from the feds after doing ten years. J. Diggs originally went down for the same case as Mac Dre and Kilo Kurt. Dre got five, Kurt got eight, and Diggs got a decade. JD, as we call Diggs, is a Crestside rider. Back in the day, he was high rollin' heavy. My cousin Pug used to hang with him, and they would let me hang out. Diggs used to rap by the name JD the Money Maker, and when I was kickin' it with him, I saw that he was all about making money. I always respected his gangsta, and when he took his fall, we stayed in contact. Before he got out, he vowed to dead the beef between me and Mac Dre, and he chose his homecoming to be where we would squash the funk.

When he first told me about the idea, I was like, "Fuck that." I didn't want to end shit. I felt like the dude betrayed me, and I wasn't about to let that slide. But Diggs and a couple of turf OGs were able to convince me to consider it. The main reason I came to the table to squash the drama was that Mac Dre and I, regardless of whether we liked it or not, were connected. We were the two figureheads of the Country Club Crest, and our turf was the womb that bore many boss macks. The fact is that we couldn't let our personal differences fuck up the main goal, which was to represent the Triple C's for the world to see.

J. Diggs's homecoming party was held on a yacht he chartered to cruise the Bay. All the Crestside cutthroats were there: Romper Room, Crew Thang, the 535 and other Crestside creepers, and the Cuttedettes (female cutthroats). It was a real 'hoodtastic event.

Before I got there, I didn't know what to think. I was expecting the best, but I prepared for the worst. When I finally arrived, it was kind of intense for a minute, but Diggs and Razor, a Romper Room OG, got Dre and I on the boat deck, and we didn't go back until we stomped out our problems. We yelled, cussed, and fussed until it was resolved. Now, I'm not gonna say that we were back brothers, but at least we could be cordial with one another and do what we had to do: represent the turf.

The cruise was fly. Dre and I got on the mic and rocked it like we used to do at Crestside 'hood house parties. When I started back recording, I did songs with Dre and Diggs, and Dre and I talked about recording a record called Da US Open. I wrapped up the record and mastered it at Studio 56. My longtime cuddie Ray Luv had also finished a monster CD, so I had asked him about putting it out on Sessed Out. Ray was with it and agreed to put his next record out on Sessed Out Records. Ray decided to call his record A Prince in Exile. I called my record Mackin' Speaks Louder Than Words. I shouldn't have to explain why. I named the CD and got ready to get back on my grind.

At first, shit was all good, but it soon got grimy. My relationship with Leila went from bad to worse, and after the record was released, for the first month and a half, I didn't even talk to my Sessed Out Records staff. Talk about shooting yourself in the foot. For real, I don't even have an excuse for my actions back then; they were just plain foolish. I mean, even if I was heated with Leila, I still should have handled my business. But like I said, hindsight is twenty-twenty, and money had me blind to the fact. I thought I was getting back at Leila by not handling my business, but what I really was doing was leading myself more astray from my life's path. Yeah, when I fuck up, I really know how to fuck up. You can just

MY OPINION

imagine how the record did with me being in Nevada on some Fear and Loathing in Las Vegas shit.

Ray Luv stayed in my ear, telling me to come back to the Bay or at least visit more. He would stay in my ear, telling me the Bay was home base, and from home base, we could take on the world. That was real talk, serious business, and the more he told me that, the more it made sense. It was like I was running in the fast lane trying to claim fame while some of the bosses of the field were trying to get in my line of work. Now, that's funny, but I wasn't laughing, 'cause the joke was on me.

I started to come back to the Bay and record songs with Ray Luv, and I started trying to get my mind back in music mode. The broad felt my focus was shifting; I figured she felt I was on my way back to the Bay, so she tried to distract me by showing out, but she could never get a rise out of me. She knew that she could never hurt my heart, so she attempted to hurt my pockets. To make a long story short, she tried to catch me in a twist by putting a simp in my mix. Then when I wouldn't flinch, the busta and a bitch put the pigs in the shit. Yeah, it surprised me that the broad would enlist the services of a sucka and they would cross one of the main rules of the game—"Don't snitch!"—just to get a reaction out of mackin'.

Now, I knew that since the sucka played ball foul, he would eventually get benched or ejected from the game completely (jailed or killed) I put the word out that the herb was a nerd and chilled, 'cause it's hard to last long with "sucka" stamped on ya dome. I decided to teach the broad a real life lesson. I easily conned her into coming back, but since the po pos knew my slave name and were on my dick, I hopped on the way, accompanied by this snake bitch who crossed me with revenge on my mind and a twinkle in my eye. I was going back to the Bay!

My fifth record, Mac'n Speaks Louder than Words

MY OPINION

Mac Dre, J-Diggs and Mac Mall at J-Diggs welcome home yacht party, this was an important night.

CHAPTER 7

THE RIDE BACK to the Bay was funny as hell. The chick was shook up. She knew she fucked up and didn't know if I was gonna bury her in the desert or what, but I had more of a diabolical fate in mind for her. When I got back to the Bay, I hit the streets running. I set up shop in San Francisco and proceeded with my plan. I was gonna show this remedial broad how we deal with faulty females in the concrete jungle. I played every track in Frisco, never giving the broad a break. No sleep, just enough food to live—man, I literally had this chick's feet bleeding. She was terrified of the Bay, 'cause out here, man, the Game is played hard and fast. She would be on the track like a deer caught in the freeway, but I didn't give a fuck. She just had better have my bread. I was gonna use her till I used her up and then throw her in the gutter.

While I was getting grimy with the chick, my cuddie Ray Luv was trying to get me on the right path. He formed a rock band called Crime Scene and made me a member of the group. He started to record tracks and do shows. I also got the line on a half-hoe hopeful who was tryin' to pay a fee to see. It's funny how shit works out. Here I was in pimp hell, tryin' to take years off this dummy's life, when out of the blue, a beezie with a stack of G's wanted to choose me. Yeah, if my life is one thing, it is eventful. I had a decision to make: do I finish torturing this idiot, or do I look at this new opportunity from the mack God? I chose the second option and came up with a play to shake the dead weight.

I had made plans to go to Chicago and get down with the Canadian broad, so I told her that I would send her out there first, and when she got settled in, I would come out there. She was so spooked of the Bay that she jumped at the chance to flee to new surroundings. I think she tried to get wise before I got her on the plane, but I rocked her back to sleep and sent her on her way. Then I got straight to work on the half-hoe hopeful.

This beezie was more watered down than I was used to working with, and she wasn't much of a looker either, but I figured she would do. See, I wasn't trying to be all out like I was. I was trying to get back on the microphone and leave the hoes alone, so I figured I would use her as a sort of pimpin' patch. Quickly I recruited her, she gave me a proper choosing fee, and it was on and cracking. Between the money I had from the dummy and the scratch I got from the new recruit, I was doing all right. I had got a little spot in the 650 and started stacking my dough.

Since my Canadian dummy was in Chicago and far away from my backhand, she was trying to get her little clown on. Two weeks had passed, and she had sent money only once. I stayed cussing her ass out. She was begging me to come to the Windy City and get the money, but I had no plans to go to Chi. But I did want to get the loot before I told her bye. Still, the lame dame was a liability, so I decided I should cut my losses before I caught a case. I got another chunk of cash and then gave her the walking papers. I straight up I told her kick boulders. It amused me to hear her flip out like a fool. She boohooed, begged, and tried to bribe me to stay on my line, but I was through. Good riddance to bad trash.

Back in the Bay, all was fly. I got so much love from everybody. It felt good to be back. Ray Luv had me doing shows with our band, Crime Scene, and we started recording a record at a studio in Marin. I never made music with a band before, but I soon found out how dope it could be. We had Frank on drums, Aaron on base, Klee on guitar, and Ant Dog on vocals with me and Ray. As we recorded more songs, we started to do more shows. We did venues in Concord, San Rafael, Humbolt County, and Santa Rosa. One of the people who gave us a lot of support was one of our cuddies named Keith. I got introduced to Keith by Ray Luv. We became fast friends—even closer than Ray's other homeboys. He was one of the folks who stayed in my ear about coming back to the Bay to handle my business. Keith was a good dude.

Since I came home, we kicked it all the time and did it live.

When it came to the Game, the half hoe was doing her thing, and I was stacking everything. I learned in the Game that hoes come and go, but dough is fa sho. I had been caught badly out there before, and I wasn't gonna let that happen again. Doing the rock/rap record with Crime Scene made me fiend to do a new rap record. Since I was going in a new direction, I wanted to do something different as far as management.

With Leila's blessing, I hollered at J. King to be my representation. I had known Jay since I started, and he was always on top of his game. I liked the aggressive way he handled the music biz. He agreed to rep me and advised me to hook up with Khayree to do some more classic material. It was cool with me, so I told him make it happen!

As expected, the half-hoe hopeful fell off but not before leaving a whole lot of loot. Her departure wasn't a issue for me; she was cool, but we never had a chance. 'cause my head was somewhere else. For the first time in a long time, I was out of the Game. It might sound square, but I felt liberated, like a great weight was lifted off my back. Now I was free to focus on being Mac Mall, rapper extraordinaire. Yeah, it's funny how shit works out. I got right back in the swing of things. Jay hooked me and Khayree back up; he was juiced to do some new material with me and started making beats for me. I got my chops back while doing the Crime Scene record. Just being in front of the microphone had me happy as a fiend with a fix.

For me, it was nothing like the lab (studio). I also was getting back in the groove of being Mac Mall the rapper.

Ray, Keith, the rest of the cuts who ran with us, and I started hitting up everything: concerts, comedy shows, and clubs. We were painting the town red with two coats! I was starting to feel like my old self, when it was just the music and me.

Now, I can't even begin to fathom the mind of the man upstairs, but maybe being my old self was my main problem, 'cause something would happen that would change me forever. The day started out better than average. Crime Scene had a studio date, and we would be finishing up our record. When Ray and I got back to the lab, everyone was in a good mood, and the day went by quickly. It felt good to be completing the project, and the whole band was amped. Ray Luv and I wanted to hit the streets, and it just so happened that Ray had the hook at Mission Rock, a big club in Frisco. He knew the promoter and wanted to introduce me to her. Pleasure plus handling a little business—sounded like a plan to me. So we called up the cuddie Keith and asked him if he wanted to go ride out with us. Keith was always ready to party, so we all made plans to meet up at Ray's tilt (house).

After I got home from the studio, I was beat and took a power nap, but I ended up sleeping till it was almost time to hit the streets. I was awakened by a call from Keith, who said he was fifteen minutes away from my building and asked me if I was ready to dip. I lied to him and said yeah. I told him to call Ray and check on him. I hung up the phone and hopped in the shower, but I couldn't help but wonder why Keith came straight to my tilt instead of meeting at Ray's like we had planned. I shook off the thought and showered. Then I got dressed and figured he just got confused. It didn't matter anyway, 'cause we would just slide by Ray's and pick him up on the way to the club.

Keith called and said he was outside, so I went out to meet him. When I got outside, I saw that he wasn't driving; it was one of his patnas who I'd met a couple times. I didn't trip, 'cause I figured Keith wanted to get torn up and didn't want the responsibility of being chauffer. I hopped in the green Lexus and fired up a back wood as we went to pick up Ray Luv. Keith was just as happy as I was that we finished the Crime Scene project, and he was ready to celebrate like he was a part of the band.

We snatched Ray Luv up; he was running late, 'cause he also fell asleep after the studio. After a little wait, he came down and we headed to Mission Rock. When we go there, we saw that it wasn't cracking like it usually was, so we decided to go to this other club we knew about in Frisco on Bay Street called Club Bass.

Now this club was crackin'; we got straight in and started showin' out. I ordered a round of Remy and Red Bull and hit the dance floor. Like I said, being home in the Bay was dope. The thugs gave it up, and the ladies gave me love. I popped at a sexy little number who was just my type. Ray had to pull me away so that we could take some flicks and order another round. I was happy! I remember telling Keith how he was my real folk, and we were laughin' and living it up. I don't know whose idea it was to leave and go back to Mission Rock, but before I knew it, Keith was telling me, "Let's go." I was the last one to get in the car, 'cause I was trying to have some people follow us to Mission Rock. As I got in the car, Ray said something funny about me being hyphy. I said something smart back, and the car was all laughs.

We turned down about three streets then hit Embarcadero. I sat back in my seat and thought about being back home and how there was no place like it. Now, this part is sketchy for me, 'cause I must have blacked it out, but I do remember the car speeding up but everything around us moving slowly. I also remember looking at Ray and then at Keith and wondering why we were going so fast. Next thing I knew, the car was getting sideways, and I was saying in my head "Oh shit!"

Then everything went blank. Some people say that when you have a near-death experience, you see your life flash in front of your eyes, but I tell you, I didn't see anything but black. When I came to, all I saw were stars in the sky, and I was sure that I was dead, but for some reason, I wasn't sad. I just tripped on how pretty the stars were and nonchalantly wondered if I would go to heaven or hell.

The first thing to let me know that I was alive was the screams I heard when I came to, and I thought, "Shit, we must have wrecked the car—but I ain't in the car; I'm in the middle of the fuckin' street! We must have been thrown from the fucking car! Shit, my fuckin' head hurts, and it feel like something stabbed me! I can feel my legs, so I guess I can walk. Let me try to walk… fuck, my side hurts, and my head is pounding! Aww, shit, where is my brother Ray?

Where the fuck is Ray?"

See, Ray and I are like brothers, and brothers feel responsible for each other. I looked for Ray in a panic and saw his body almost a block up the street. He was laid out on the corner near Pacific Bell Park. I became more alarmed when he wasn't moving. I yelled his name, but he was knocked out. I yelled his name again, and he woke up. Seeing him moving relieved me a little, but he was in bad condition. His head was busted, and when he tried to get up, he couldn't. The only traumatic events in my life before then had been shootings, so when I heard him speak, I knew he was alive. Then all of a sudden, like it was an explosion in my head—"Keith!"

Where was he? I didn't see him around us. I got up to find him. I looked up the street and saw a crowd forming. I walked up the street as best as I could and saw the driver of the car all bloody. His face was caved in, his leg was broken in three places, and he was all mangled and tangled in an iron fence. I heard him moan and thought he must still be alive. OK, where the fuck was Keith?

Then I looked farther up the street and saw Keith lying there, motionless, and a lady was kneeling next to him. I limped over to him and yelled his name, but he didn't move. It was all still a blur, but I could see that his head was busted badly. The lady told me to take off my shirt and wrap his head. I did as I was told, even though I was in shock. The lady also told me to talk to Keith and try to keep him awake, so I grabbed his hand and said, "Keith. Fight, Keith! Cuddie, this Mall. I'm with you, cuddie. I'm with you! Fight, cuddie. Fight!"

By this time, a crowd formed, and peopled called the police, but I couldn't even notice all the chaos going on around me. All I could see were Keith's eyes. His eyes were fighting to stay open, fighting for life. It took the police to pull me away from him so that the ambulance could get through to work on him. I was in a complete daze. This couldn't be real.

When the cops started questioning me, I snapped out of it, and my street sense took over. The roller (police) asked what happened, and I said, "I don't know. I wasn't in the car." When I said that, he looked at me like I was crazy and said, "Sir, I can tell by your appearance that you were in the car. What happened?" I guess I was in shock, but I didn't even notice that my head had been split open and was bleeding heavily and that my jacket was ripped to shreds. I was fucked up.

They quickly put Keith, Ray, and the driver in ambulances and took them to the hospital. They told me to get in an ambulance, but I tried to tell them I was OK and didn't need one. Once they told me I'd die if I went home and went to sleep, I decided I'd better go to the hospital so they could check me out. We all got taken to the San Francisco General Hospital ER. It was like a madhouse; you had people in there who had been shot, stabbed, and burned. The broken up, beat down, overdosed, comatose, blind, crippled, and crazy—from old folks to babies—were all in there, all in different states of anguish.

They split us up and began to work on us. I couldn't tell where they put Keith and the driver, but they put Ray across the hall from me. I could hear him talking in the other room, so when the doctors stopped working on me, I limped over to his room.

The first thing we said to each other was "what the fuck happened?" Just like me, Ray didn't know what went down. I told him that we must have wrecked. I told him how messed up Keith and the driver were. Then we just sat there dumbfounded, not knowing whether to cry or cuss. Finally they split us up again, 'cause the doctors wanted to finish checking us out.

While the doctors looked me over, I got on the phone with my mom and Leila and let them know what happened. I also called my homegirl Kawanna because honestly besides my mom and Leila I didn't have anyone else to call.

As I layed in the hospital bed, I felt numb, mentally and physically. I knew I was injured, but I felt no pain. I knew I had been a part of a disaster, but I layed there stupefied.

All of a sudden, the doctor came in with a somber look on his face. Just by looking at him, I could tell that he was gonna tell me that somebody was dead; I just didn't know who he was gonna say passed away. I remember it word for word. He said, "Jamal, I got some bad news to tell you. Your friend Keith didn't make it (make it, make it make it)." Damn. I knew Keith was in bad shape, but I didn't know the extent of his injuries.

MY OPINION

All the shit felt like a nightmare, and I almost thought I'd wake up, and Keith and Ray would be standing in front of me OK, talking about the plans we had for the night. But this wasn't a bad dream; this was reality, and like I said, reality bites like a fucking pit bull! Since I was the only one who could stand, when Keith's folks got to the ER, I gave Keith's father the rundown. I could barely look Keith's pops in his eyes, 'cause they held the look of pain I couldn't describe.

After I told Keith's pops what happened, I went back in the room they had me in; Kawanna was waiting in there for me. I could tell by the look in her face that I must have looked like a zombie, 'cause that's how I felt: dead inside. Kawanna was cool though, she held my head while a nurse hey put nine staples in it and then went to Ray's room and comforted him while he got worked on.

They ran a couple of tests on me to make sure I didn't have any internal bleeding and then basically told me I could go. Still in a daze, I told Ray that they were making me leave; I didn't want to go, though. I didn't feel it was fair that I could go home, and Keith would never be able to, and Ray wouldn't be going home anytime soon, 'cause they said he broke his hip and fractured a vertebra in his back.

It was crazy, though, 'cause Ray was in worse shape than me, but he was worried about how I was doing. I guess he could see that I was hurt more in my mind than

I was physically. He and Kawanna said that I should go home and rest my battered body and mind. I agreed to leave but told Ray to call me when he got to his room. The ride home was eerie. I didn't talk to Kawanna at all. It was daytime, so I just looked at the sky and the clouds and the sun. Throughout my life, I put myself in situations where I almost got myself killed.

You know, getting shot at and other street shit like that.

When I was little, I almost choked to death and even almost drowned. I don't know what to say, though—this time was different. Maybe it was because not only did I almost die, but I watched my friend fight for his life and lose. I was confused. I mean, I was trying to do right. I was out of the Game, and all I was doing was music. Why did this bullshit have to happen to me? A fuckin' car wreck! No doubt I was happy to be alive, but I didn't understand why my friend Keith had to die. I didn't know the driver well, but I think that karma wise, I probably had more bad shit coming my way, but Keith's family was the one who had to mourn. I can't lie; I was feeling guilty for surviving the accident.

Kawanna took me home and stayed with me for a while, but my mind was somewhere else. I kept having flashbacks of the night before. I kept seeing Ray all bloody, the driver all bloody, Keith fighting for his life, and his eyes—his blue eyes. When Kawanna left, I took

MY OPINION

some pills that I got from the hospital, layed in the bed, stared at the ceiling, and thought, "Why? Why did this have to happen to us?"

After an uneasy sleep, I called the hospital and hollered at Ray. He was in the room, all drugged up, but he still tried to talk to me. Man, Ray and I had been through a whole lot of crazy shit through the years, but I knew this event would test us individually. I felt ashamed to talk to him, 'cause I was at home, and he was at San Francisco General with tubes in him.

I felt fucked up—fucked up in the head and the body. My back was so bad that I couldn't even move. The pills they gave me didn't do shit. All I could do was sit there and think about what went wrong. I also thought about life, my family, my turf, and my music. I thought about everything important and how it almost got snatched away from me in a blink on an eye. For the first time, I actually saw how fragile how life was.

The days went by, but my mind stayed in one place, one time, and one night. I replayed the events of that night over and over in my head and tried to figure out if I could've done something differently to change the outcome. But every time I thought about it, it played out the same. I went to see Ray a couple of times in the hospital. His grandmother was there all the time. She was a very beautiful, religious, kindhearted lady. She prayed for Ray and me and even the driver. Her unshakable faith somehow eased my mind a little. Ray was lucky to have her there. The doctor tried to tell Ray that he might be in the hospital for six months, but Granny's prayers seemed to go straight to Gods ears, 'cause Ray healed quicker than the doctors expected. When the day came for K-DOE's (Keith's) memorial, Ray and I went together with Alex (a close friend of both of ours), Ray's grandmother, and his son. It was a beautiful service.

There was no casket—just a picture of Keith. Everyone who knew and loved Keith got up and said a few words. The next day, along with Keith's family, we went out on a yacht and scattered his ashes under the Golden Gate Bridge.

It was hard for me to look into the eyes of Keith's parents and his girlfriend, Bianca, but I had to ride to the end for my cuddie Kato. I spent the months after Keith's funeral mostly alone, reflecting.

Shit, it's like I lived two lifetimes. I rose to glory from grime, and I overcame obstacles that were put in front of me and obstacles that I made for myself. I've been a sometimes saint, part-time devil, fate's fool, and king of contradiction. I grazed greatness but also made many mistakes. I've been dope, but I've also been dumb. I've been ambitious, but I've also been irresponsible. I made lifelong friends but also gained eternal enemies. I spent a lot of time and energy chasing material bullshit that would have been divvied up among my family if I would have died in the crash. Yeah, I've been a fool, but you know they say: God protects babies and fools. I used to think that it was my cleverness that got me out of those crazy situations, but I see I only survived through the grace of God, and if he or she kept me alive through all the drama, and I still have my sanity, then I must be here for a reason. I guess living is finding out what that reason is.

Eventually I came to peace with the accident. You see, God don't make any mistakes, and my friend Keith is in a much better place. Now I know that his eyes that used to haunt me are there with my ancestors, watching over me.

I had to go through hell and back to get on the right track, but I can't look back at anything I've been through or done as a mistake, because I learned from it. Yea, I didn't go to college, but I got a doctorate from the school of hard knocks. I'm not saying that I'm reformed or that I've got all the answers, but I see now that you've got to look at life's race like a marathon and not a sprint. It's about living, not just existing. It's about fulfilling your destiny and taking advantage of every moment, 'cause man, time ain't money, though fools stay trying to tell you that. You can lose and gain money, but you could never salvage a second.

I'm not proud of all that I've done, and I don't want to glamorize the deeds that I did. You've gotta know that the lessons learned on the streets came with a price. See, I could have been getting further on my life's path. I'm not saying that I didn't get far, but let's say I went a long way to get a short distance. But man, I'm alive.

I'm stronger, I'm wiser, I've got my sanity and my health, and I'm focused on dropping records like rabbits drop bunnies. I'm back in the studio with Khayree and feeling the passion about music, like I did when I was at my mom's kitchen table. I treasure my friends and family more, because I know they are the most important things in the world, and in the end, that's all you've got. I just respect myself and my life more than I did, and I thank God for everything that I've seen.

It's true that what doesn't kill you makes you stronger, and I do feel stronger. Yeah, I never ran from God's dealt hand. I played this life-or-death game the best way that I could, jumped off life's cliff, and didn't care where I landed. I learned lessons, even when God's plan changed my plans. Through bad, good, losses, and wins, here I stand as a Mac among men…and that's my opinion.

MY OPINION

My homeboy Keith from Santa Rosa, aka K-Doe

Keith and his woman Bianca

MY OPINION

Me, Keith, Ray Luv (and the driver) the last pic we took before we got into a car and got into a fatal accident.

ACKNOWLEDGEMENTS

MY MOM AND POPS at first it was hard for y'all to understand my dream but I'm happy that I'm able to make you proud

MY BROTHER IMMANUEL I love you and I'm proud of you

MY AUNTIES and COUSINS I love all y'all

TO MY BIOLOGICAL FATHER
This book was written about my past
We have the future to make thing right lets do it

MY SISTERS AND LITTLE BROTHER I love y'all

THE COUNTRY CLUB CREST couldn't of been raised anywhere better it's in us not on us 3CDOWN

THE MAC thank you big Cuddie (CREST IN PEACE)

MAC DRE glad we was able to get it right Cuddie I'm gone keep it lit (CREST IN PEACE)

DJ CEE thank you for being our glue (CREST IN PEACE)

KHAYREE we change the game and we did it together thank you

LEILA thank you for holdin my hand through this crazy game love you

RAY LUV you already know brother

KARLA thanks for being the first ears to hear this and letting me know I could do it

PHILMORE GRAHAM thank you (REST IN PEACE)

FOSTER HICKS thank you for teaching me

MY MY FANS thank you for rockin with me for many moons I do it for y'all and we not done it's just the beginning much love

MAC MALL CONTACT INFORMATION
EMAIL Macdamos@gmail.com
INSTAGRAM @therealmacmall
TWITTER @therealmacmall

www.ingramcontent.com/pod-product-compliance
Lightning Source LLC
Chambersburg PA
CBHW070948180426

43194CB00041B/1801